LOGIC
PUZZLES

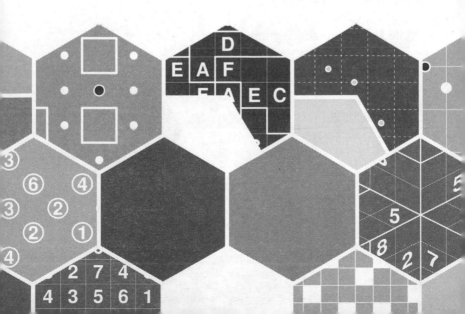

Published in 2023 by Welbeck
An imprint of Welbeck Non-Fiction Limited
part of Welbeck Publishing Group
Offices in: London – 20 Mortimer Street, London W1T 3JW
& Sydney – 205 Commonwealth Street, Surry Hills 2010
www.welbeckpublishing.com

Puzzles and Design © 2022 Welbeck Non-Fiction,
part of Welbeck Publishing Group

Editorial: Tall Tree Limited
Design: Tall Tree Limited and Eliana Holder

All rights reserved. No part of this publication may be
reproduced, stored in a retrieval system, or transmitted
in any form or by any means, electronically, mechanical,
photocopying, recording or otherwise, without the prior
permission of the copyright owners and the publishers.

A CIP catalogue for this book is available from the British
Library.

ISBN: 978-1-80279-670-4

Printed in the United Kingdom

10 9 8 7 6 5 4 3 2 1

FSC
www.fsc.org

MIX
Paper | Supporting
responsible forestry
FSC® C171272

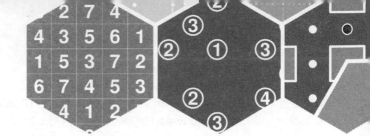

LOGIC PUZZLES

More than 150 brain teasers to test your
powers of deduction

Dr Gareth Moore

WELBECK

INTRODUCTION

Welcome to this challenging collection of logic puzzles, packed from cover to cover with over 165 puzzles of 16 different types. Some of the puzzles in the book may already be familiar, such as sudoku, but for those types that are new to you then the rules for that puzzle are always given at the start of the corresponding chapter. Read those instructions carefully and make sure you understand how they apply to an actual puzzle. If anything is unclear, don't be afraid to take a look at a solution of that type (at the back of the book) so you can see how they correspond to the finished grid. There's no point getting started while being confused over the instructions, after all!

Within each chapter, the puzzles generally get trickier as you work through that chapter, often evolving into larger and less-heavily clued versions of that type as you progress. This means that it's best to start at the beginning of a chapter, rather than dip in randomly, although it doesn't matter which chapter you start at since the puzzle types themselves are ordered for variety rather than intrinsic logical complexity of that type.

Remember that for the best mental benefit it's important to try puzzles that challenge you, so don't just skip over the types that seem particularly tricky – give them a good go and your brain is sure to thank you for making the effort!

Best of luck with the puzzles, and remember to have fun!

Dr Gareth Moore, London

FENCES

INSTRUCTIONS
Join all of the dots to form a single loop. The loop cannot cross or touch itself at any point. Only horizontal and vertical lines between dots are allowed. Some parts of the loop are already given.

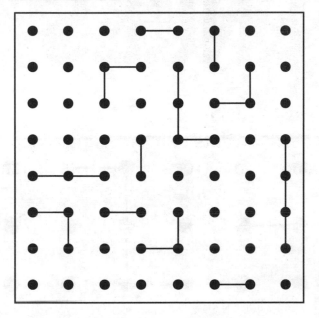

SOLUTION

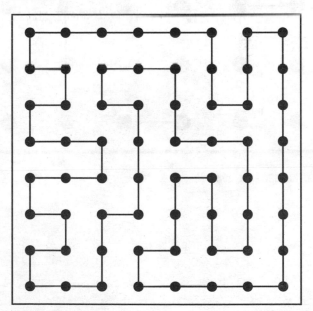

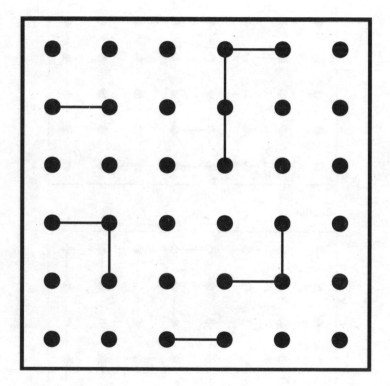

SOLUTION SEE PAGE 204

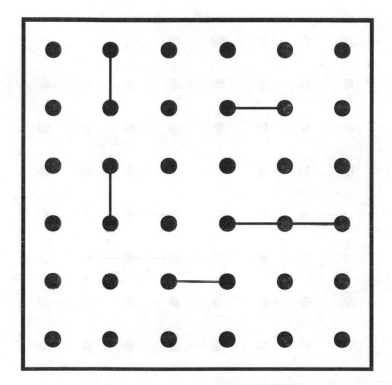

SOLUTION SEE PAGE 204

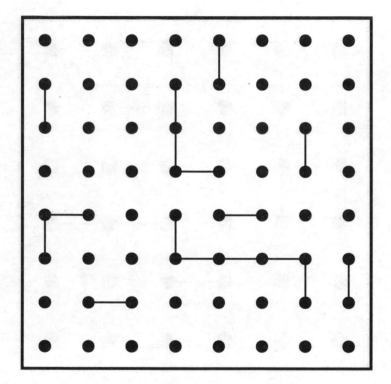

SOLUTION SEE PAGE 205

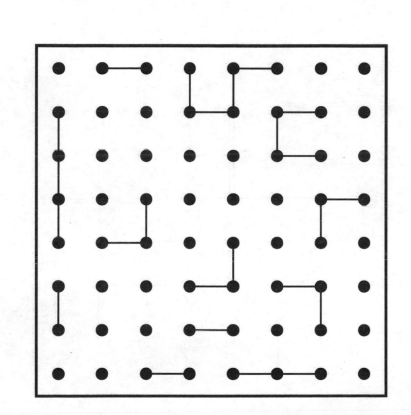

SOLUTION SEE PAGE 205

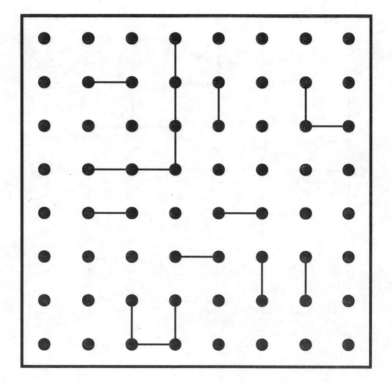

SOLUTION SEE PAGE 206

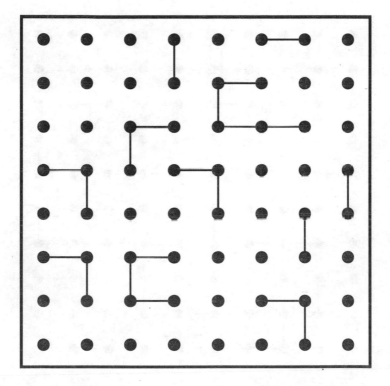

SOLUTION SEE PAGE 206

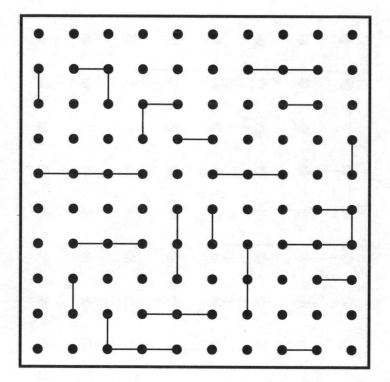

SOLUTION SEE PAGE 207

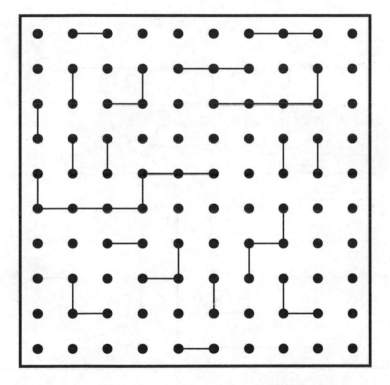

SOLUTION SEE PAGE 207

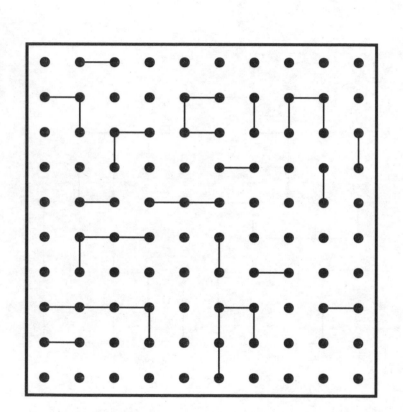

SOLUTION SEE PAGE 208

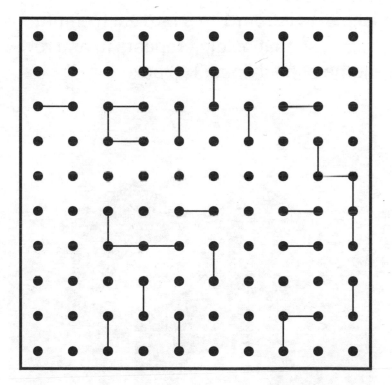

SOLUTION SEE PAGE 208

SUDOKU

INSTRUCTIONS

Place a digit from 1 to 9 into each empty square, so that no digit repeats in any row, column or bold-lined 3×3 box.

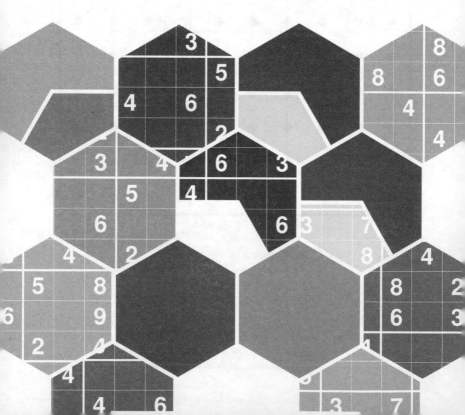

EXAMPLE

7			5		8			1
		8		9		3		
	5			1			2	
4			8		1			5
	6	9				1	8	
2			6		9			4
	2			6			7	
		3		4		5		
6			7		5			3

SOLUTION

7	9	2	5	3	8	6	4	1
1	4	8	2	9	6	3	5	7
3	5	6	4	1	7	8	2	9
4	3	7	8	2	1	9	6	5
5	6	9	3	7	4	1	8	2
2	8	1	6	5	9	7	3	4
9	2	5	1	6	3	4	7	8
8	7	3	9	4	2	5	1	6
6	1	4	7	8	5	2	9	3

	6			4			8	
3			8		2			5
	8		6		3		4	
9		4				5		8
1			4		6			9
6		5				2		4
	9		3		7		5	
7			1		8			6
	1			2			7	

SOLUTION SEE PAGE 209

8				4	3			6
					2	3		
							7	5
6	8		1					
	9		4		7		1	
					9		4	3
1	7							
		9	5					
3			6	9				7

SOLUTION SEE PAGE 209

7	6						5	3
9			5		6			4
	7			5			4	
	3		8	9	7		6	
			3		2			
	9						8	
2								1
4			2	1	3			6

SOLUTION SEE PAGE 210

5								7
		6		5		2		
	1		3		8		4	
		3	5		2	8		
	2						3	
		1	4		9	7		
	9		7		5		1	
		4		8		3		
1								6

SOLUTION SEE PAGE 210

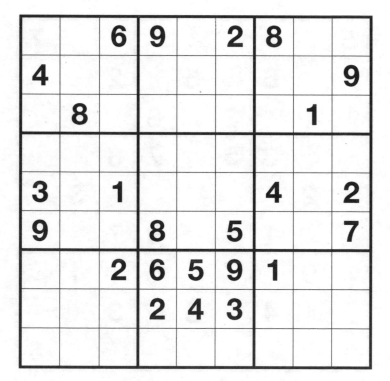

SOLUTION SEE PAGE 211

		8		2		7		
			8	4	1			
4								6
	8		6		9		2	
9	4						6	3
	2		5		4		1	
1								2
			4	6	5			
		3		1		6		

SOLUTION SEE PAGE 211

8	9						1	3
	2		6		1		7	
9			8		4			2
		4	7	1	6	9		
1			9		3			8
	4		3		7		2	
7	1						8	6

SOLUTION SEE PAGE 212

	9				6		5	
5			3		7			9
		3		5		7		
1	3						2	
		9				3		
	7						8	1
		7		2		4		
2			9		4			5
	5		6				7	

SOLUTION SEE PAGE 212

8					2		3	
		7			5		4	
					9		1	7
			2			3		5
4		2			8			
6	7		5					
	2		6			1		
	5		3					4

SOLUTION SEE PAGE 213

			6	1	9			
	4						5	
2			4		3			8
8				2				4
		9	1		6	3		
3				8				2
		4		9		1		

SOLUTION SEE PAGE 213

SHAPE LINK

INSTRUCTIONS

Draw a series of separate paths, each connecting a pair of identical shapes. No more than one path can enter any square, and paths can only travel horizontally or vertically between squares.

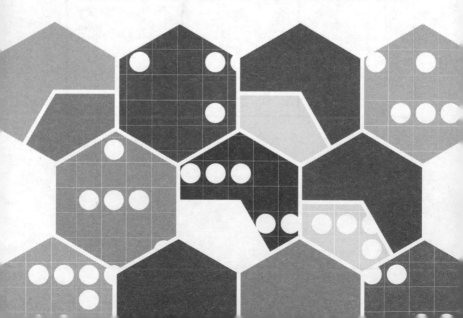

EXAMPLE

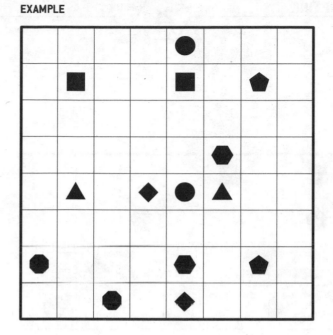

SOLUTION

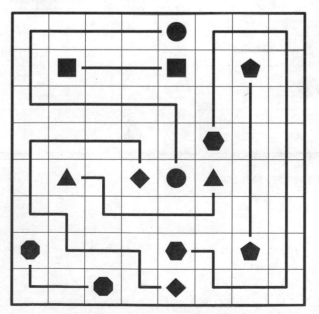

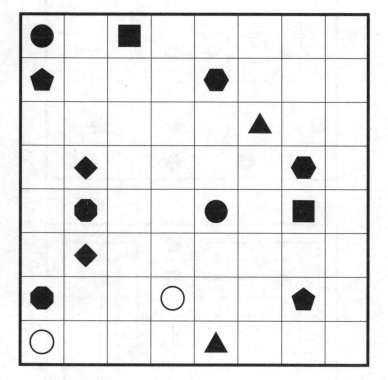

SOLUTION SEE PAGE 214

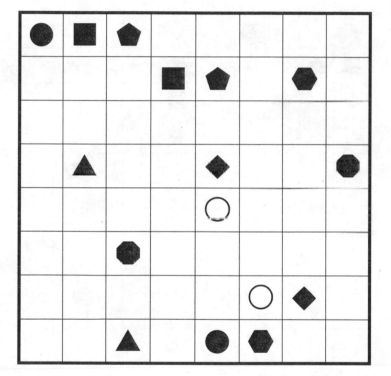

SOLUTION SEE PAGE 214

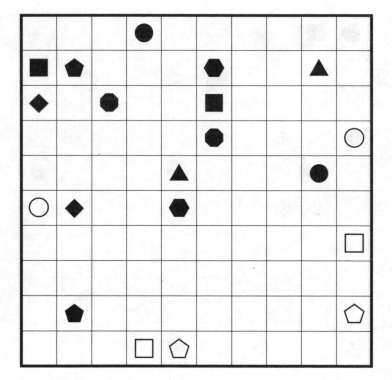

SOLUTION SEE PAGE 215

SHAPE **LINK**

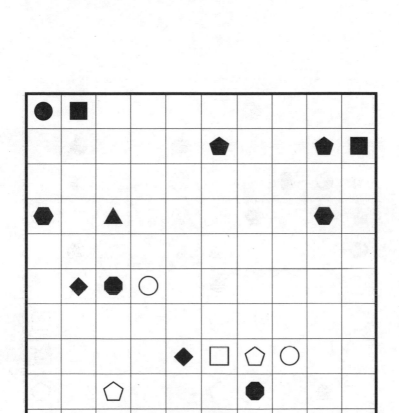

SOLUTION SEE PAGE 215

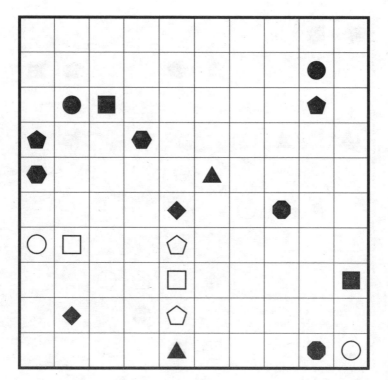

SOLUTION SEE PAGE 216

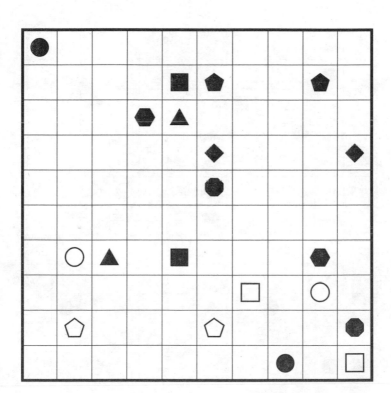

SOLUTION SEE PAGE 216

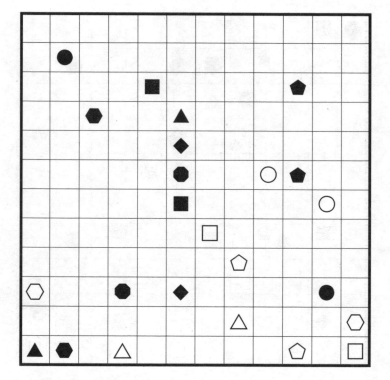

SOLUTION SEE PAGE 217

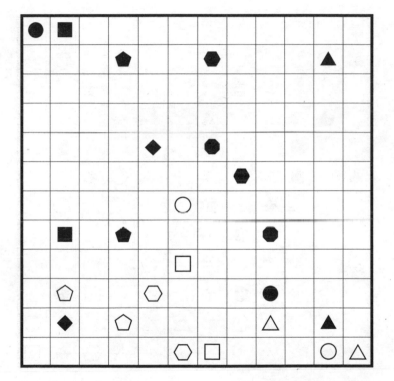

SOLUTION SEE PAGE 217

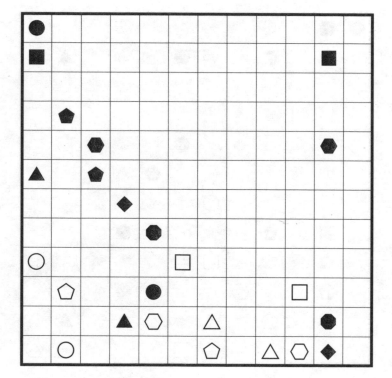

SOLUTION SEE PAGE 218

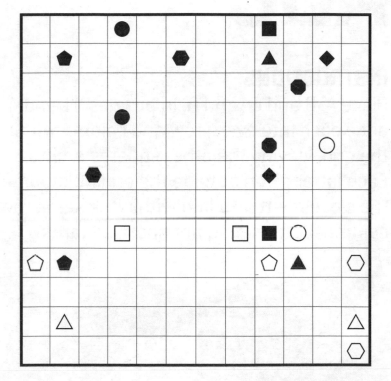

SOLUTION SEE PAGE 218

EASY AS ABC

INSTRUCTIONS

Place A, B and C (and D, in puzzles 41 and 42) once each into every row and column within the grid, leaving the other squares empty. Each letter given outside the grid must match the closest letter to it in within the same row/column. Letters may not share squares.

EXAMPLE

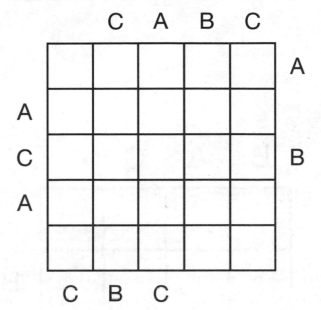

SOLUTION

	C	A	B	C	
B	C	A			A
A			B	C	
C			A	B	B
	A	B	C		A
	B	C		A	

C B C

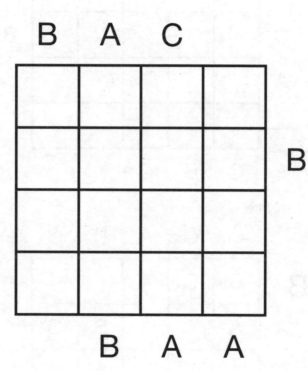

SOLUTION SEE PAGE 219

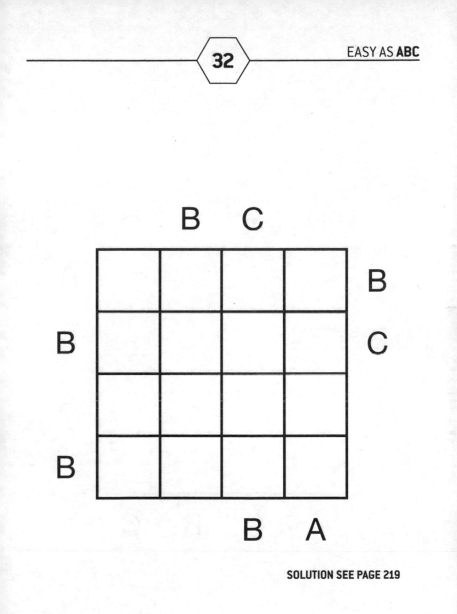

SOLUTION SEE PAGE 219

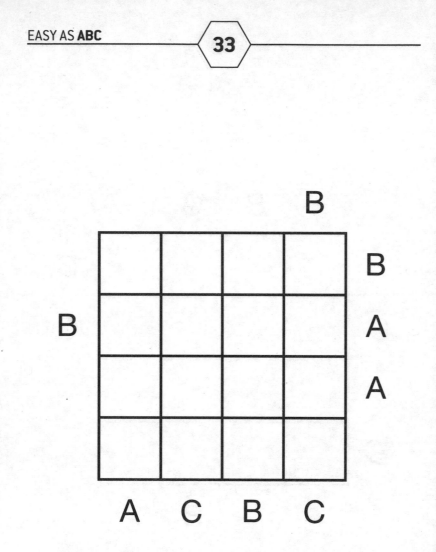

SOLUTION SEE PAGE 220

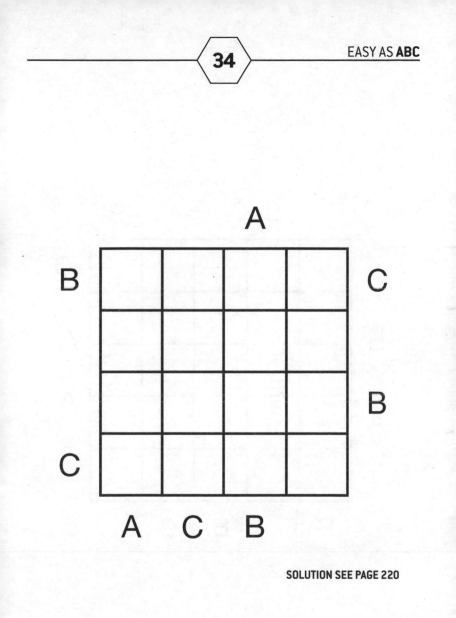

SOLUTION SEE PAGE 220

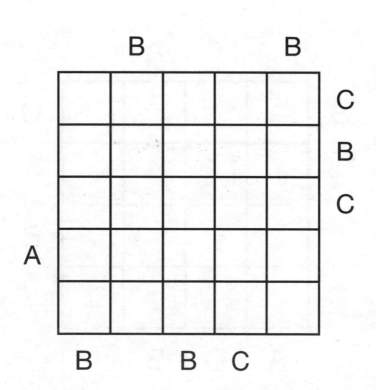

SOLUTION SEE PAGE 221

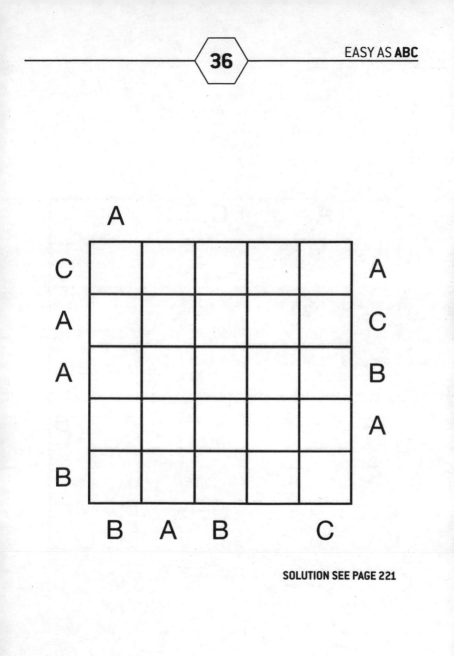

SOLUTION SEE PAGE 221

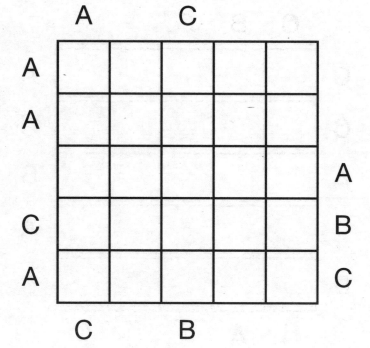

SOLUTION SEE PAGE 222

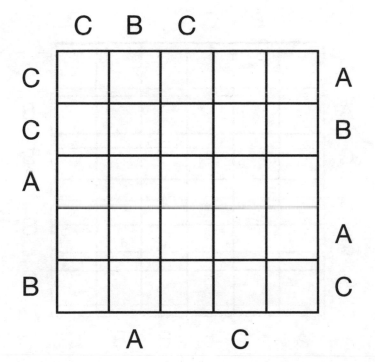

SOLUTION SEE PAGE 222

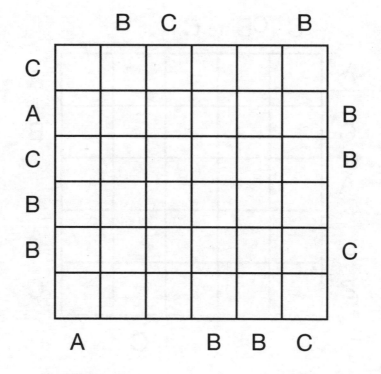

SOLUTION SEE PAGE 223

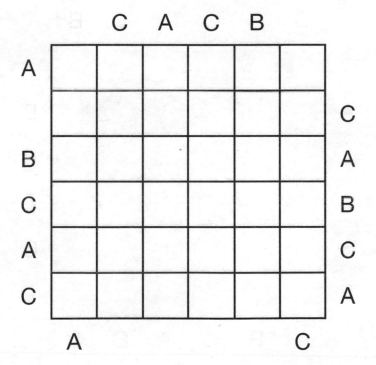

```
          C   A   C   B
      ┌───┬───┬───┬───┬───┬───┐
  A   │   │   │   │   │   │   │
      ├───┼───┼───┼───┼───┼───┤
      │   │   │   │   │   │   │   C
      ├───┼───┼───┼───┼───┼───┤
  B   │   │   │   │   │   │   │   A
      ├───┼───┼───┼───┼───┼───┤
  C   │   │   │   │   │   │   │   B
      ├───┼───┼───┼───┼───┼───┤
  A   │   │   │   │   │   │   │   C
      ├───┼───┼───┼───┼───┼───┤
  C   │   │   │   │   │   │   │   A
      └───┴───┴───┴───┴───┴───┘
        A               C
```

SOLUTION SEE PAGE 223

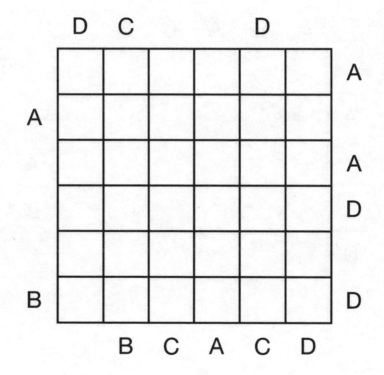

SOLUTION SEE PAGE 224

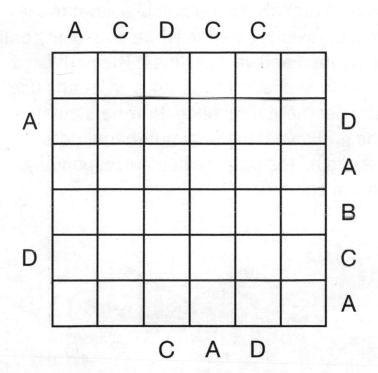

SOLUTION SEE PAGE 224

LINE FIT

INSTRUCTIONS

Draw a path that joins one black dot to the other, travelling via the white dots using only horizontal and vertical lines. The path can't cross any shaded squares, and it can't use any dot more than once. Numbers outside the grid reveal the total number of dots visited by the path in their corresponding row or column.

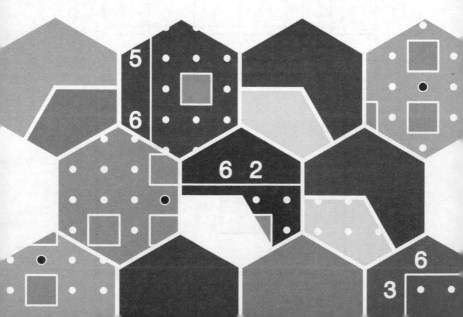

EXAMPLE

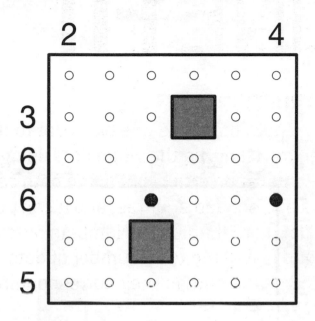

SOLUTION

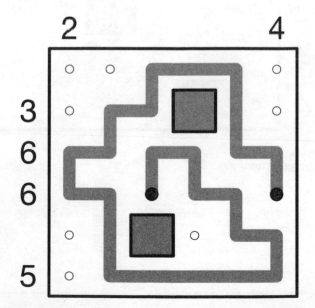

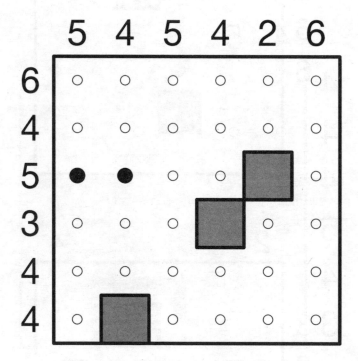

SOLUTION SEE PAGE 225

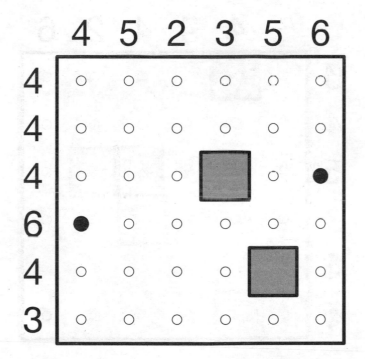

SOLUTION SEE PAGE 225

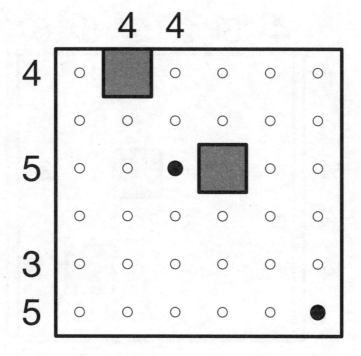

SOLUTION SEE PAGE 226

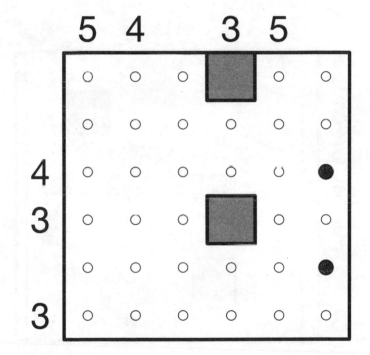

SOLUTION SEE PAGE 226

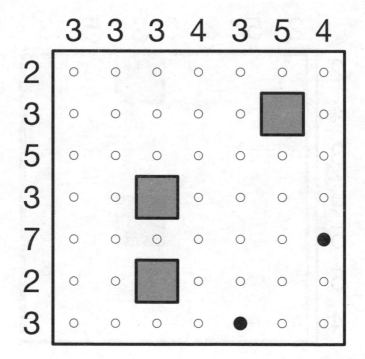

SOLUTION SEE PAGE 227

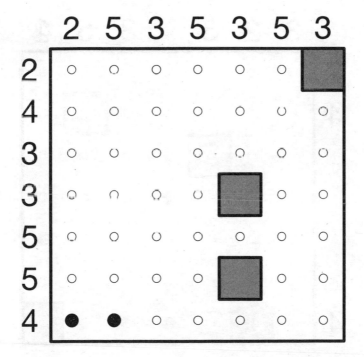

SOLUTION SEE PAGE 227

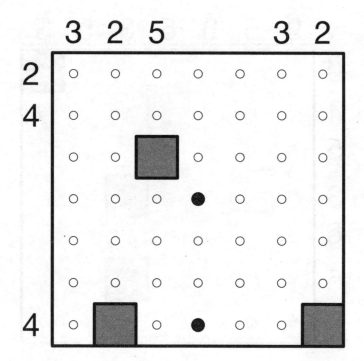

SOLUTION SEE PAGE 228

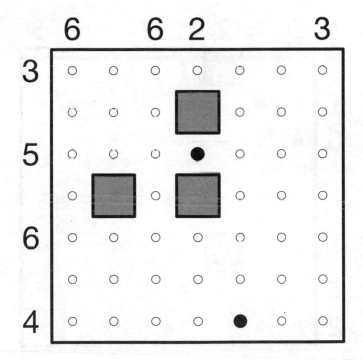

SOLUTION SEE PAGE 228

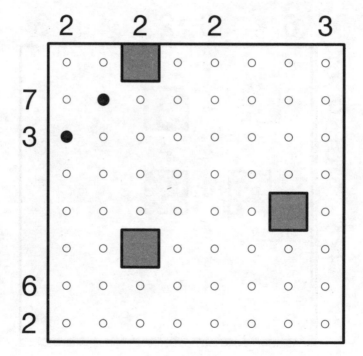

SOLUTION SEE PAGE 229

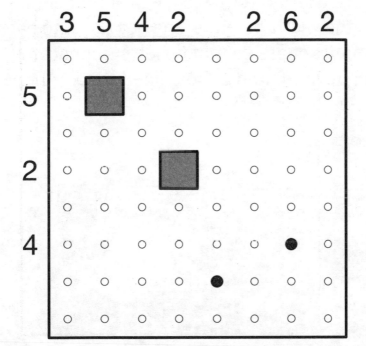

SOLUTION SEE PAGE 229

JIGDOKU

INSTRUCTIONS

Place a letter from A to F, G or H (depending on the width/height of the puzzle) into each empty square so that no letter repeats in any row, column or bold-lined jigsaw shape.

EXAMPLE

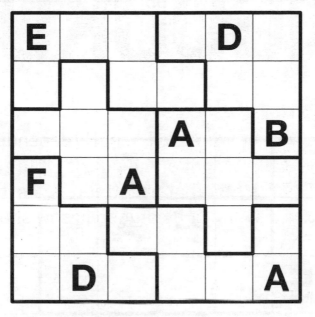

SOLUTION

E	A	B	C	D	F
C	B	F	D	A	E
D	F	E	A	C	B
F	C	A	E	B	D
A	E	D	B	F	C
B	D	C	F	E	A

SOLUTION SEE PAGE 230

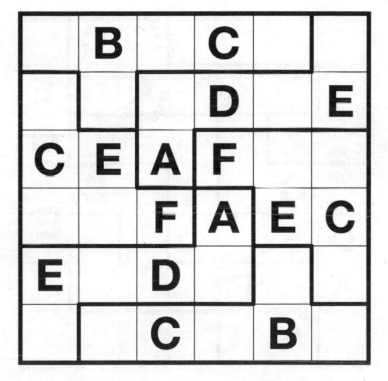

SOLUTION SEE PAGE 230

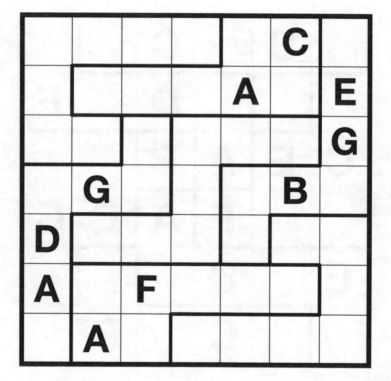

SOLUTION SEE PAGE 231

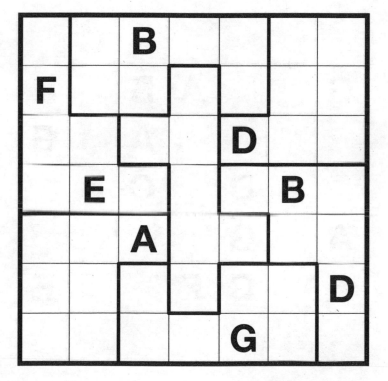

SOLUTION SEE PAGE 231

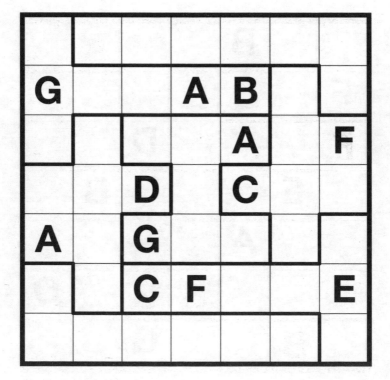

SOLUTION SEE PAGE 232

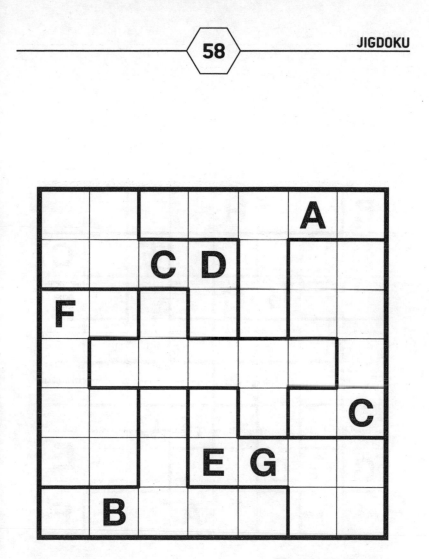

SOLUTION SEE PAGE 232

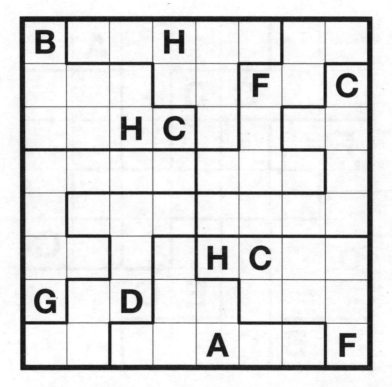

SOLUTION SEE PAGE 233

SOLUTION SEE PAGE 233

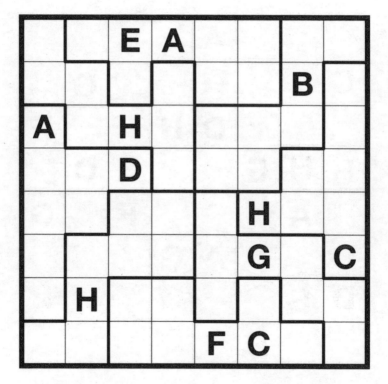

SOLUTION SEE PAGE 234

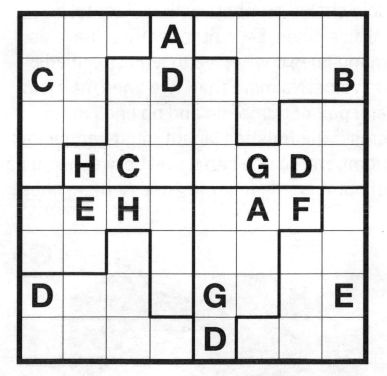

SOLUTION SEE PAGE 234

BRIDGES

INSTRUCTIONS

Join circled numbers with horizontal or vertical lines. Each number must have as many lines connected to it as specified by its value. No more than two lines may join any pair of numbers, and no lines may cross. The finished layout must connect all numbers, so you can travel between any pair of numbers by following one or more lines.

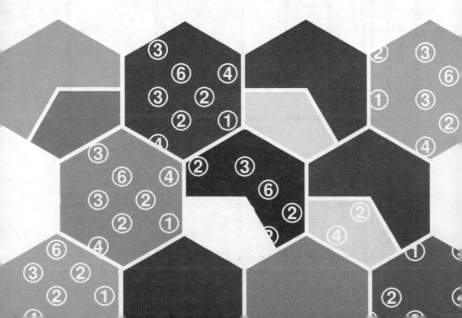

EXAMPLE

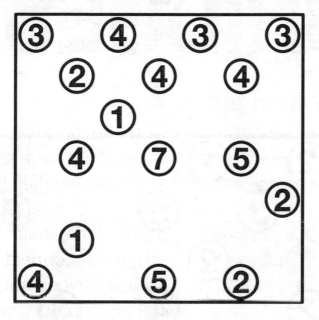

SOLUTION

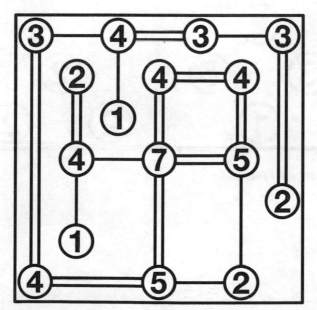

SOLUTION SEE PAGE 235

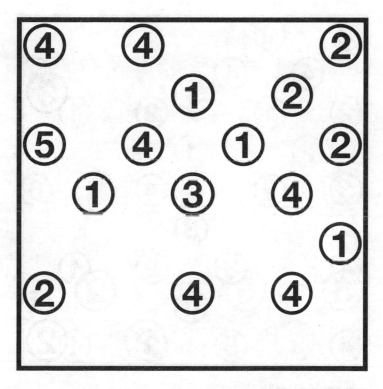

SOLUTION SEE PAGE 235

SOLUTION SEE PAGE 236

②　　③　　　　⑤　　　　③

　　①　　　　②　　　　②

②

　　　②　　③

　③　　　　⑥　　④

②　　①　　③　　②　　④

　　　　　②　　①

　②　　　④　　　　②

③　　③　　　　　①

SOLUTION SEE PAGE 236

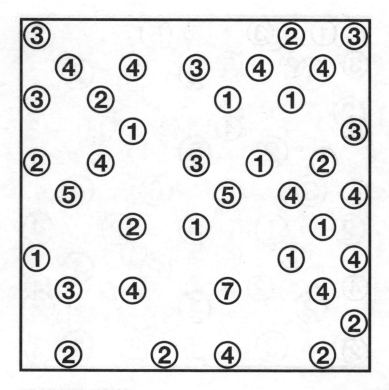

SOLUTION SEE PAGE 237

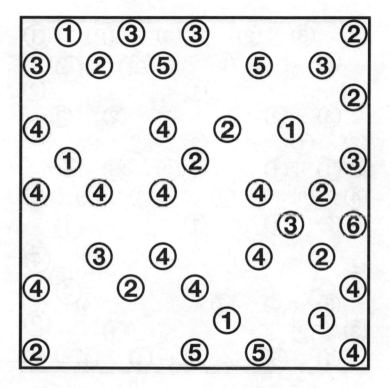

SOLUTION SEE PAGE 237

③ ③ ② ③ ② ①
③ ⑥ ⑤ ②
① ②
③ ② ② ③
② ① ② ③
① ① ② ⑤ ④
④ ⑥ ⑧ ③ ② ③
② ① ①
① ③ ④
② ②
③ ④ ③ ④ ⑥
③ ② ①
① ③ ③ ④ ④ ③

SOLUTION SEE PAGE 238

SOLUTION SEE PAGE 238

SOLUTION SEE PAGE 239

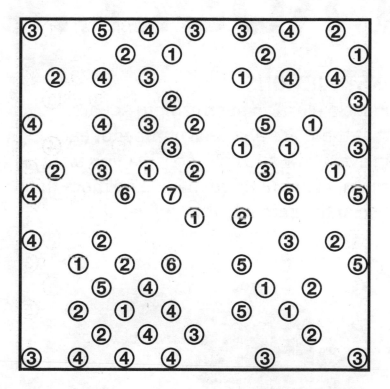

SOLUTION SEE PAGE 239

BINARY
PROBLEM

INSTRUCTIONS

Place a 0 or 1 in every empty square so that there are an equal number of each digit in every row and column. Reading along a row or column, there may be no more than two of the same digit in succession.

EXAMPLE

	0	1	0				1
			1	0			1
	1	1				0	
		1		0	0		1
1		0	0		1		
	0				1	0	
0			1	1			
1				0	1	0	

SOLUTION

0	0	1	0	1	0	1	1
1	0	0	1	0	0	1	1
0	1	1	0	1	1	0	0
0	0	1	1	0	0	1	1
1	1	0	0	1	1	0	0
1	0	1	0	0	1	0	1
0	1	0	1	1	0	1	0
1	1	0	1	0	1	0	0

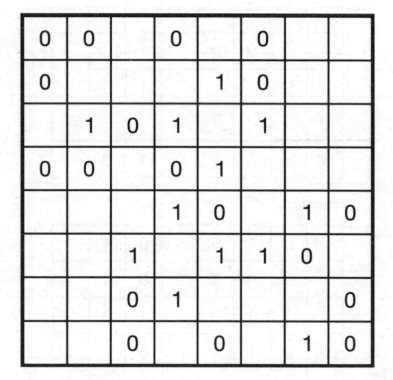

0	0		0		0		
0				1	0		
	1	0	1		1		
0	0		0	1			
			1	0		1	0
		1		1	1	0	
		0	1				0
		0		0		1	0

SOLUTION SEE PAGE 240

74

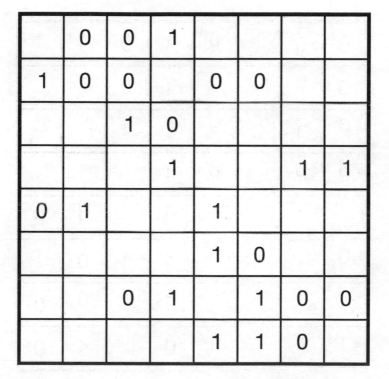

	0	0	1				
1	0	0		0	0		
		1	0				
			1			1	1
0	1			1			
				1	0		
		0	1		1	0	0
				1	1	0	

SOLUTION SEE PAGE 240

			0	1		1	1
	0	0	1			1	
0							0
0	0		0				
				0		0	0
0							1
	1			0	1	0	
1	1		1	0			

SOLUTION SEE PAGE 241

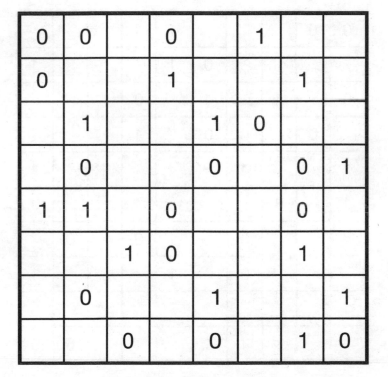

SOLUTION SEE PAGE 241

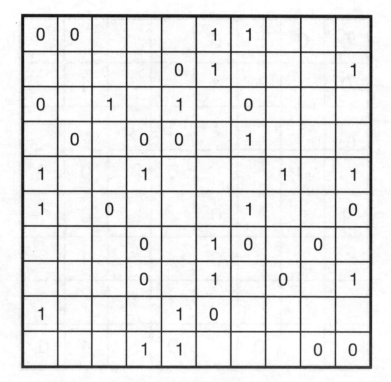

0	0				1	1			
				0	1				1
0		1		1		0			
	0		0	0		1			
1			1				1		1
1		0				1			0
			0		1	0		0	
			0		1		0		1
1				1	0				
			1	1				0	0

SOLUTION SEE PAGE 242

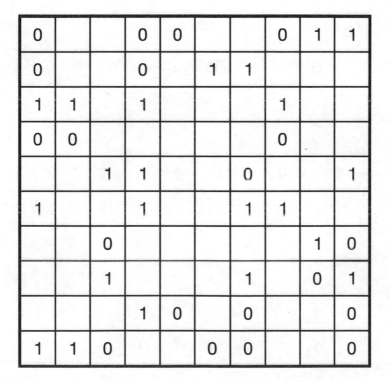

0			0	0			0	1	1
0			0		1	1			
1	1		1				1		
0	0						0		
		1	1			0			1
1			1			1	1		
		0						1	0
		1				1		0	1
			1	0		0			0
1	1	0			0	0			0

SOLUTION SEE PAGE 242

1			1		0			1	1
	0			0				1	
		1	0				0		
	0	1				1		0	
		0			1				
				1			0		
	1		0				1	1	
		1				1	0		
	1				1			1	
1	1			1		0			0

SOLUTION SEE PAGE 243

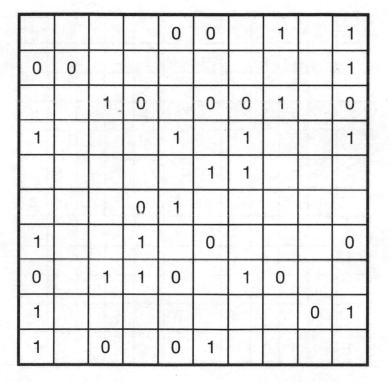

SOLUTION SEE PAGE 243

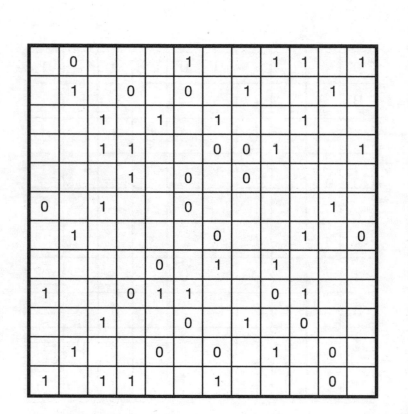

	0				1			1	1		1
	1		0		0		1			1	
		1		1		1			1		
		1	1			0	0	1			1
			1		0		0				
0		1			0					1	
	1					0			1		0
				0		1		1			
1			0	1	1			0	1		
		1			0		1		0		
	1			0		0			1	0	
1		1	1			1				0	

SOLUTION SEE PAGE 244

BINARY **PROBLEM**

0			1	0	0		0				
0								0		1	
				0			0				1
	0			1		1				0	1
0	0							1		1	
		0								1	1
1	0								1		
	1		0							1	1
1	1				0		1			0	
0			1			1					
	1		0								0
				1		1	0	0			0

SOLUTION SEE PAGE 244

KROPKI

INSTRUCTIONS

Place a number from 1 to 6, 7 or 8 (depending on the width/height of the puzzle) in each empty square, so no number repeats in any row or column. Squares joined by a white dot contain consecutive digits, meaning that they have a numerical difference of 1. Squares joined by a black dot contain digits where one is exactly twice the value of the other. If there is no dot then neither relationship applies.

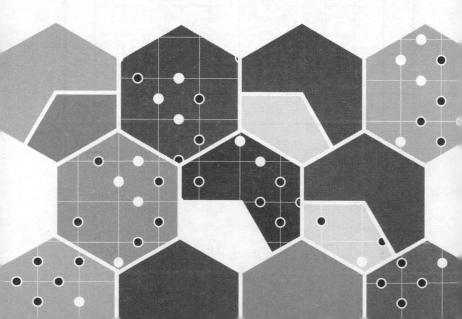

EXAMPLE

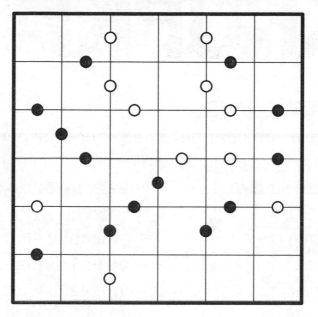

SOLUTION

1	4 ○ 5	3 ○ 2	6
6	2 ○ 3	5 ○ 4	1
3 • 6	4	1 5	2
5	3 1 • 2	6	4
4 1 • 2	6 • 3	5
2	5 ○ 6	4	1	3

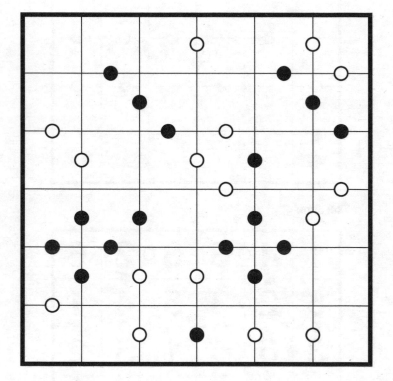

SOLUTION SEE PAGE 245

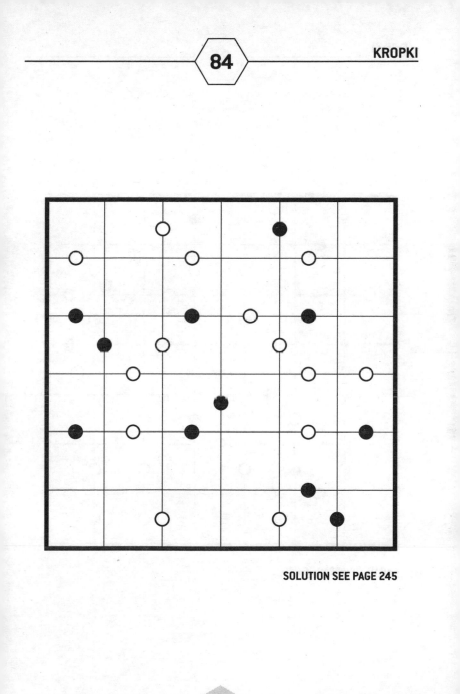

SOLUTION SEE PAGE 245

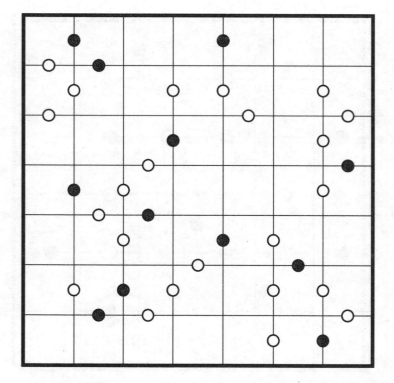

SOLUTION SEE PAGE 246

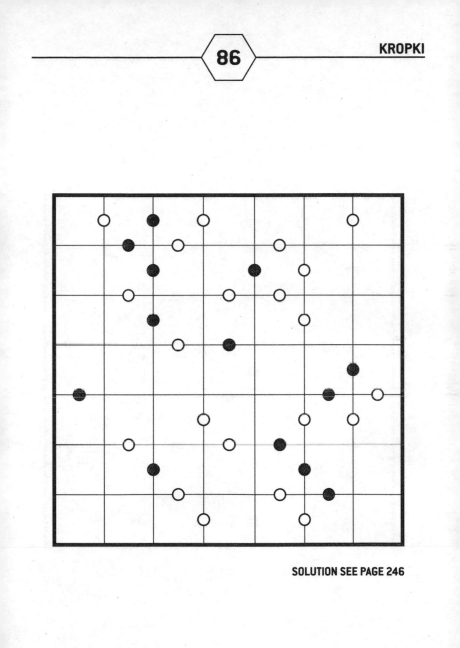

SOLUTION SEE PAGE 246

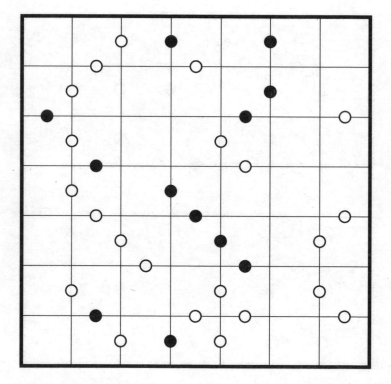

SOLUTION SEE PAGE 247

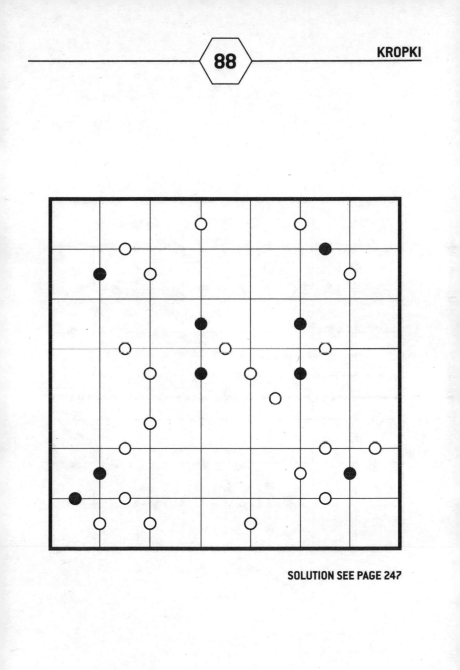

SOLUTION SEE PAGE 247

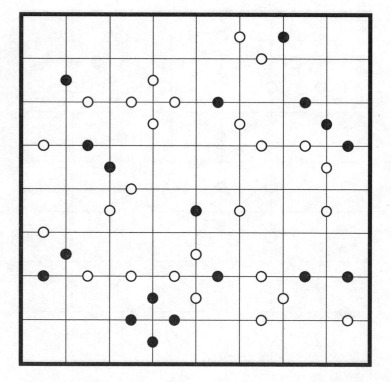

SOLUTION SEE PAGE 248

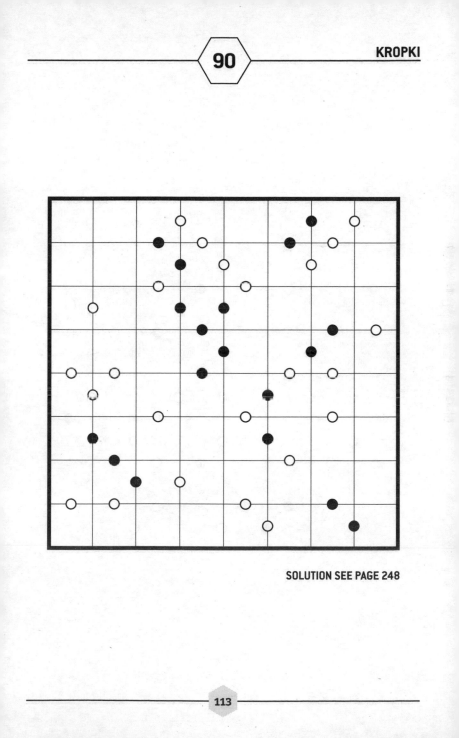

SOLUTION SEE PAGE 248

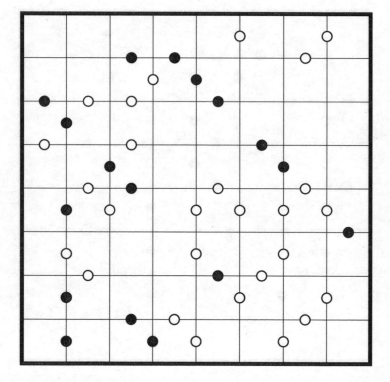

SOLUTION SEE PAGE 249

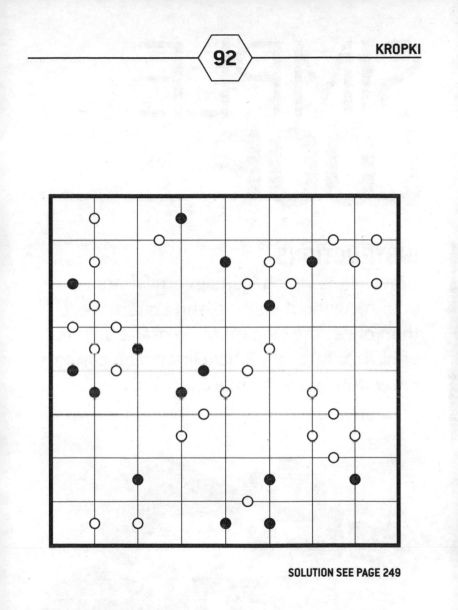

SOLUTION SEE PAGE 249

SIMPLE LOOP

INSTRUCTIONS

Draw a loop which visits every white square, without visiting any square more than once. The loop must be made up only of horizontal and vertical lines, and cannot enter any shaded squares.

EXAMPLE

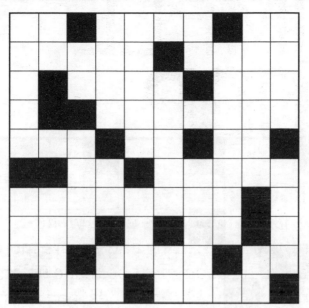

SOLUTION

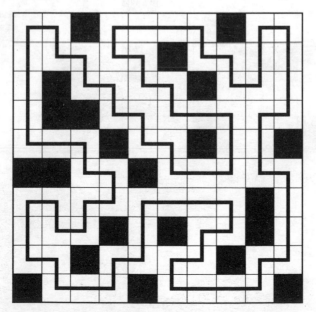

SOLUTION SEE PAGE 250

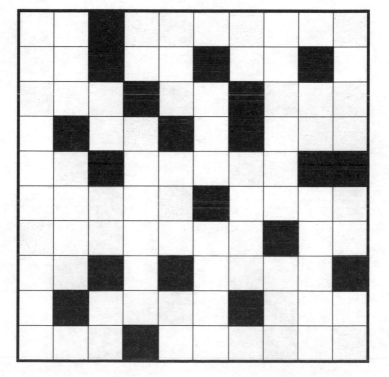

SOLUTION SEE PAGE 350

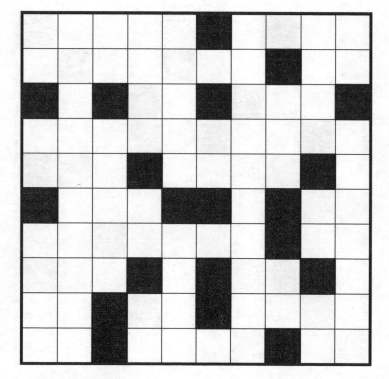

SOLUTION SEE PAGE 251

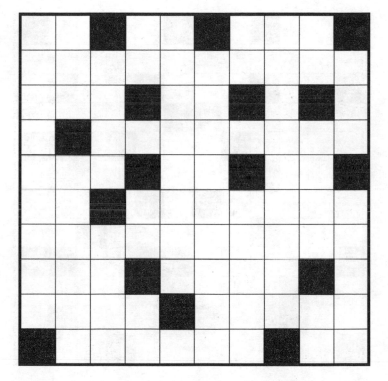

SOLUTION SEE PAGE 251

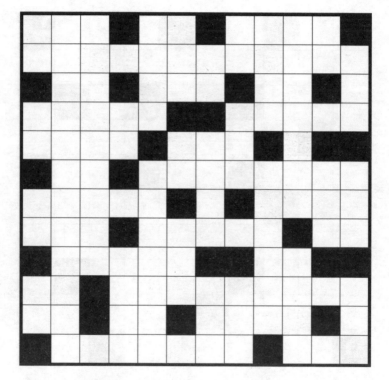

SOLUTION SEE PAGE 252

SOLUTION SEE PAGE 252

SOLUTION SEE PAGE 253

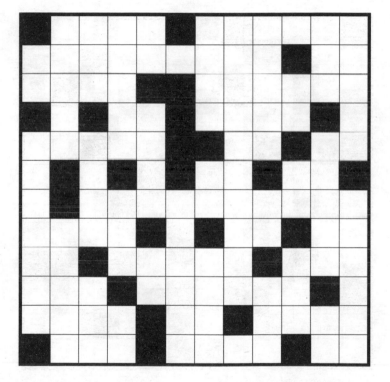

SOLUTION SEE PAGE 253

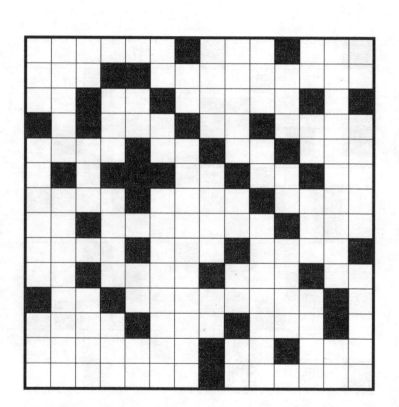

SOLUTION SEE PAGE 254

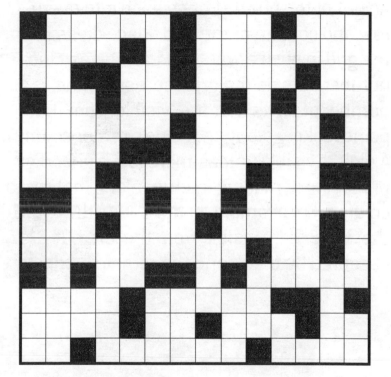

SOLUTION SEE PAGE 254

SKYSCRAPER

INSTRUCTIONS

Place 1 to 5, 6 or 7 (depending on the width/height of the puzzle) once each into every row and column of the grid. Place digits in the grid in such a way that each given clue number outside the grid represents the number of digits that are 'visible' from that point, looking along that clue's row or column. A digit is visible unless there is a higher digit preceding it, reading in order along that row or column. For example, in the 5-long row '32514' the 3 and 5 are visible from the left, but 2 is obscured by the 3, and the remaining digits by the 5.

EXAMPLE

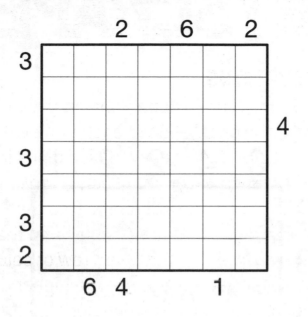

SOLUTION

	2			6		2	
3	4	3	6	7	1	2	5
	5	7	1	6	2	4	3
	7	6	2	5	3	1	4
3	2	5	7	3	4	6	1
	1	4	5	2	6	3	7
3	3	2	4	1	7	5	6
2	6	1	3	4	5	7	2

4

6   4   1

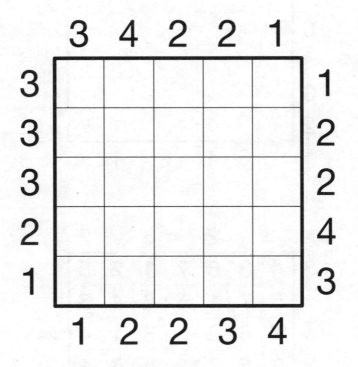

SOLUTION SEE PAGE 255

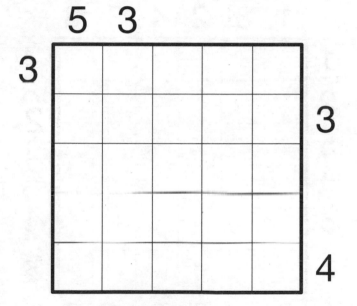

SOLUTION SEE PAGE 255

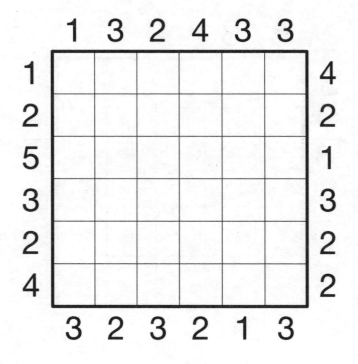

SOLUTION SEE PAGE 256

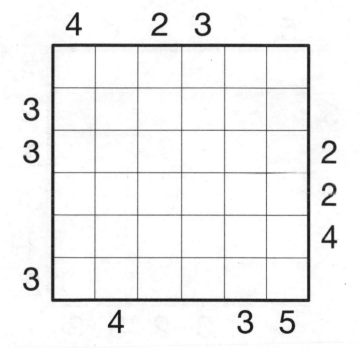

SOLUTION SEE PAGE 256

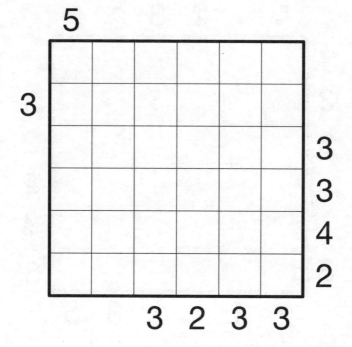

SOLUTION SEE PAGE 257

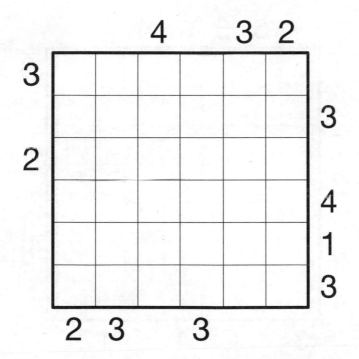

SOLUTION SEE PAGE 257

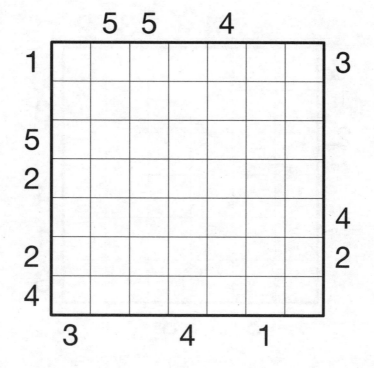

SOLUTION SEE PAGE 258

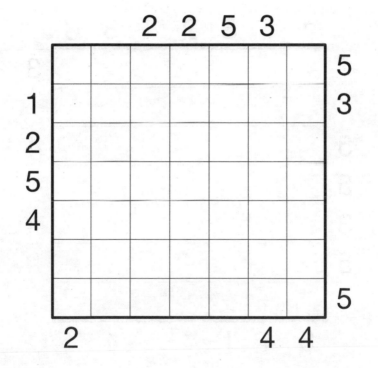

SOLUTION SEE PAGE 258

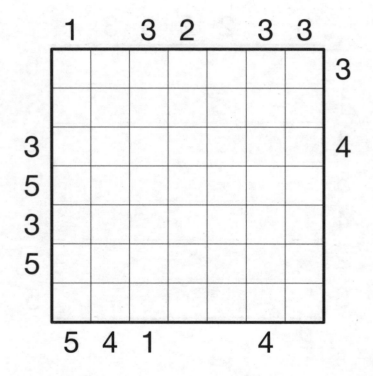

SOLUTION SEE PAGE 259

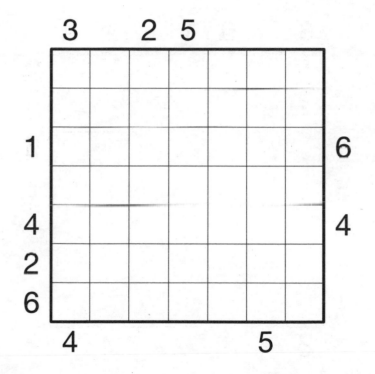

SOLUTION SEE PAGE 259

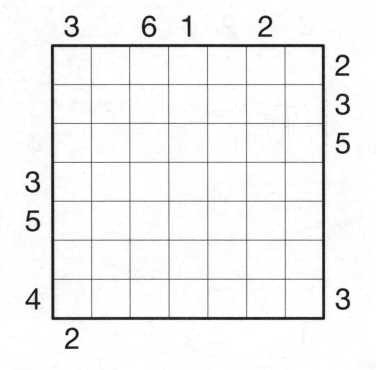

SOLUTION SEE PAGE 260

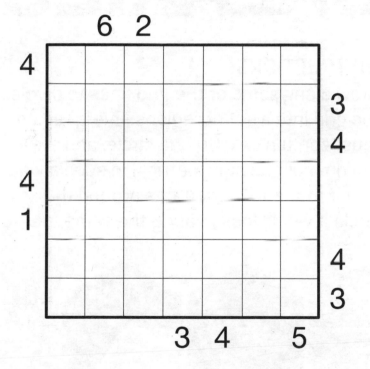

SOLUTION SEE PAGE 260

SPIRAL GALAXIES

INSTRUCTIONS

Draw along some of the grid lines to divide the grid into a set of regions. Every region must contain exactly one circle, and the region must be symmetrical in such a way that if rotated 180 degrees around the circle it would look exactly the same.

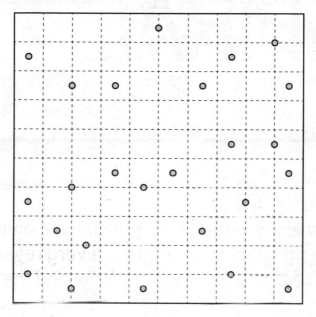

SOLUTION

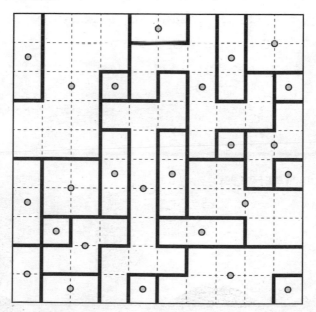

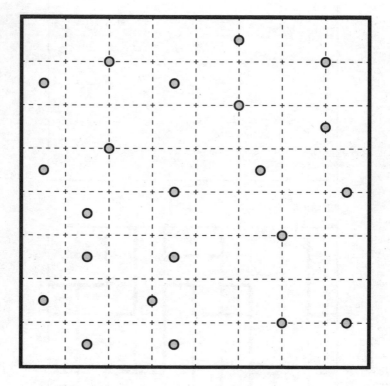

SOLUTION SEE PAGE 261

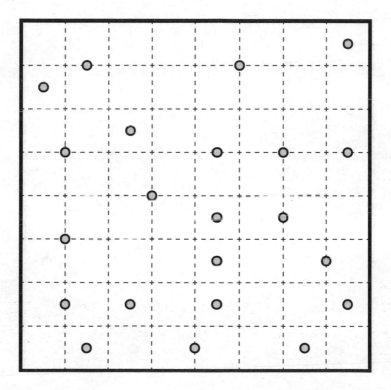

SOLUTION SEE PAGE 261

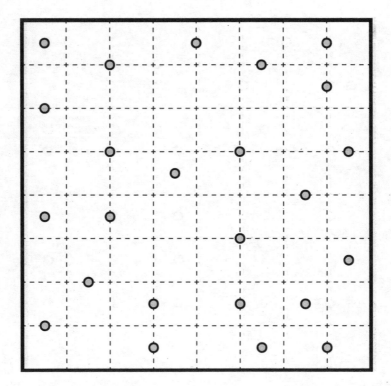

SOLUTION SEE PAGE 262

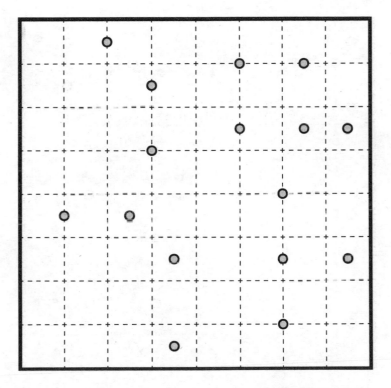

SOLUTION SEE PAGE 262

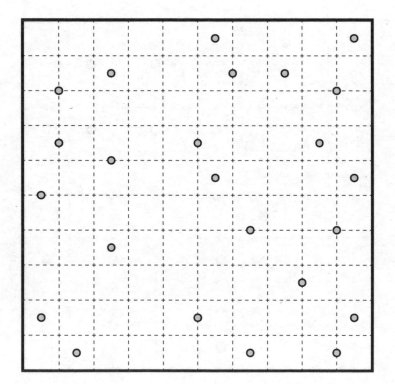

SOLUTION SEE PAGE 263

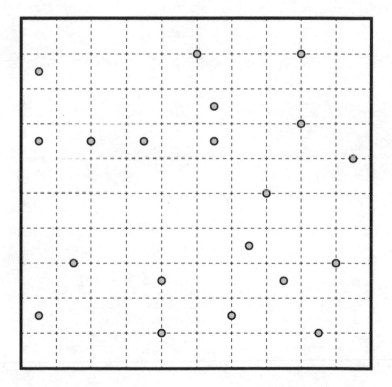

SOLUTION SEE PAGE 263

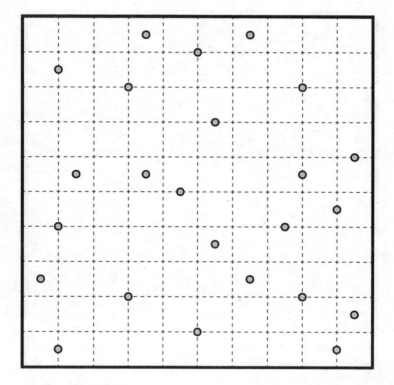

SOLUTION SEE PAGE 264

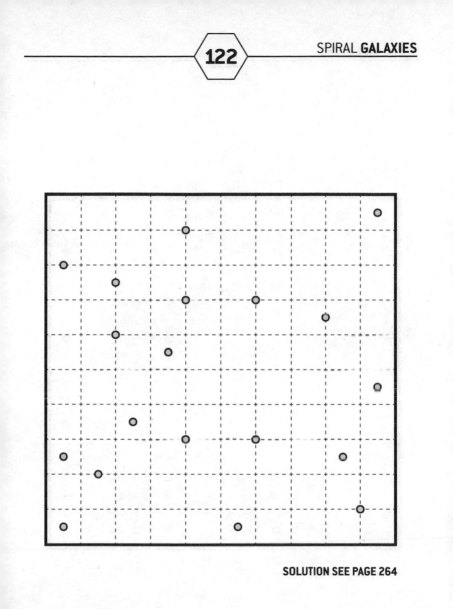

SOLUTION SEE PAGE 264

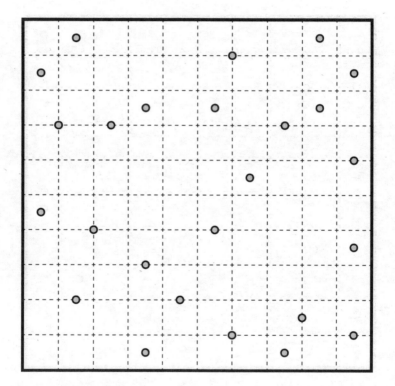

SOLUTION SEE PAGE 265

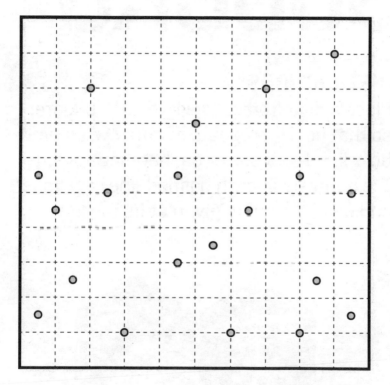

SOLUTION SEE PAGE 265

KILLER SUDOKU

INSTRUCTIONS

Place a digit from 1 to 9 into each square, so that no digit repeats in any row, column, bold-lined 3×3 box or dashed-line cage. The numbers in each dashed-line cage must add up to the value given at its top left.

EXAMPLE

SOLUTION

⌐14 3	8	⌐14 9	5	⌐15 7	2	6	⌐26 1	4
1	⌐12 7	⌐10 4	⌐12 8	⌐9 3	6	⌐5 2	5	9
2	5	6	4	⌐10 1	9	3	⌐19 8	7
⌐14 8	⌐7 3	⌐13 7	6	⌐32 5	4	⌐8 1	9	2
6	4	⌐3 2	1	9	8	7	⌐9 3	⌐13 5
⌐20 5	9	1	3	2	⌐11 7	4	6	8
⌐23 7	6	⌐13 5	⌐10 2	8	⌐4 1	⌐14 9	⌐6 4	⌐17 3
9	1	8	⌐11 7	4	3	5	2	6
4	2	⌐18 3	9	6	⌐13 5	8	7	1

SOLUTION SEE PAGE 266

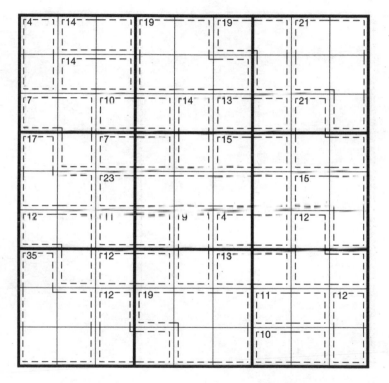

SOLUTION SEE PAGE 266

SOLUTION SEE PAGE 267

SOLUTION SEE PAGE 267

SOLUTION SEE PAGE 268

SOLUTION SEE PAGE 268

SOLUTION SEE PAGE 269

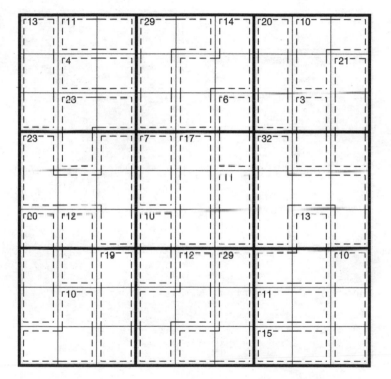

SOLUTION SEE PAGE 269

SOLUTION SEE PAGE 270

SOLUTION SEE PAGE 270

SNAKE

INSTRUCTIONS

Shade some squares to form a single snake that starts and ends at the given squares. A snake is a path of adjacent squares that does not branch or cross over itself. The snake does not touch itself – not even diagonally, except when turning a corner. Numbers outside the grid specify the number of squares in their row or column that contain part of the snake.

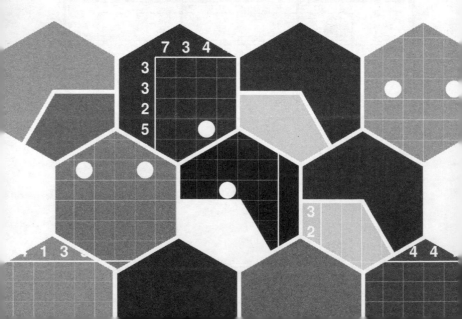

EXAMPLE

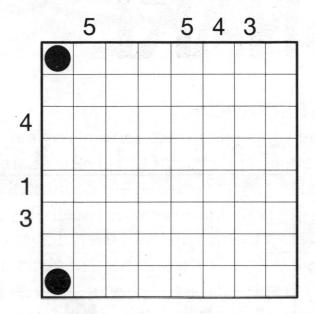

SOLUTION

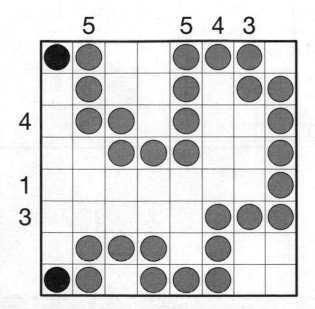

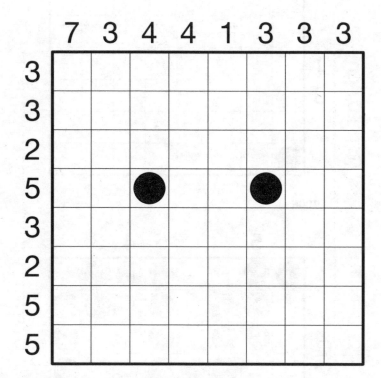

SOLUTION SEE PAGE 271

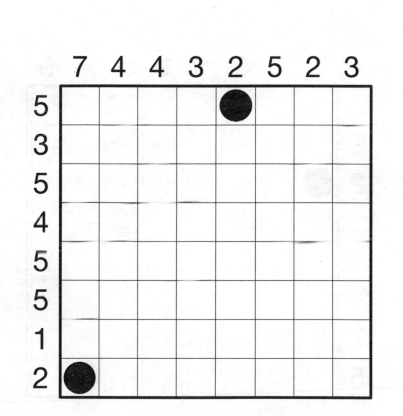

SOLUTION SEE PAGE 271

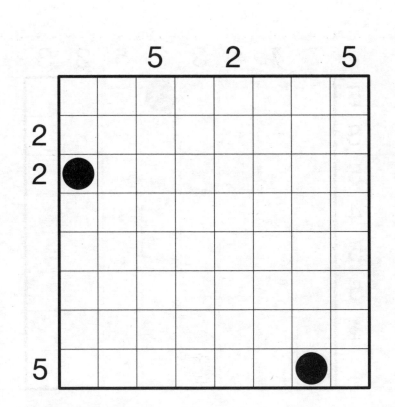

SOLUTION SEE PAGE 272

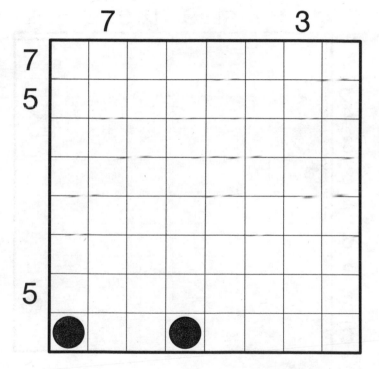

SOLUTION SEE PAGE 272

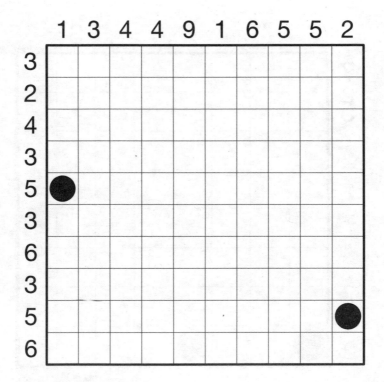

SOLUTION SEE PAGE 273

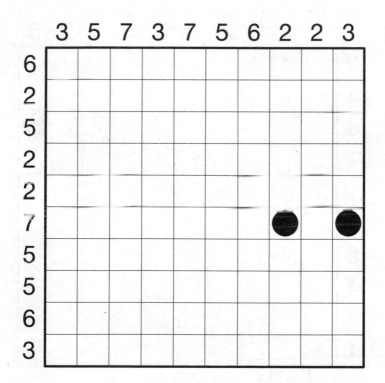

SOLUTION SEE PAGE 273

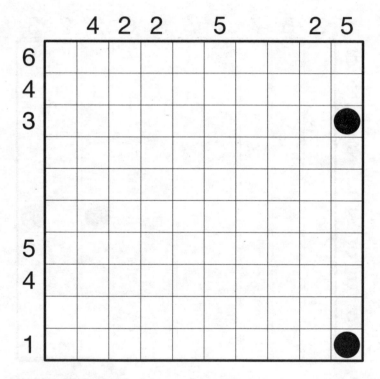

SOLUTION SEE PAGE 274

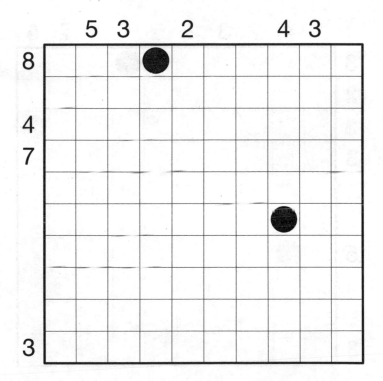

SOLUTION SEE PAGE 274

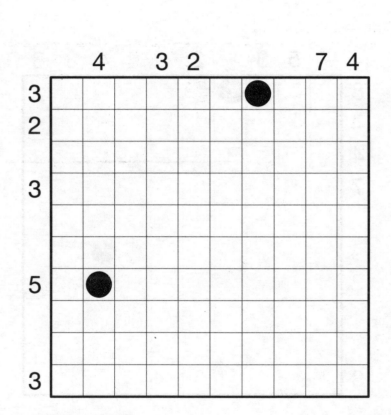

SOLUTION SEE PAGE 275

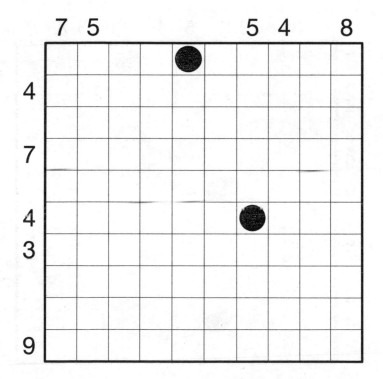

SOLUTION SEE PAGE 275

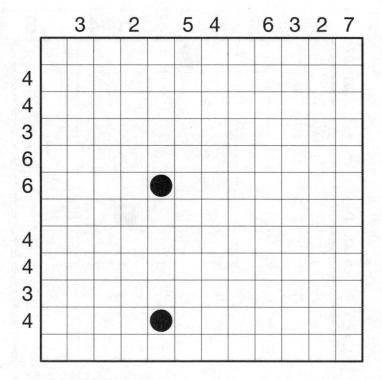

SOLUTION SEE PAGE 276

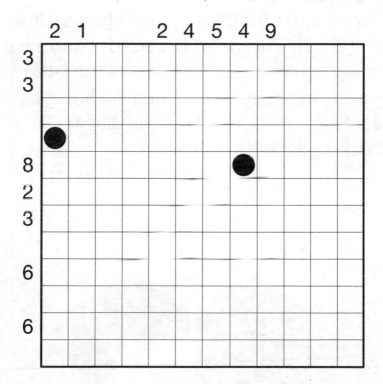

SOLUTION SEE PAGE 276

TOUCHY

INSTRUCTIONS

Place a letter from A to F, G or H (depending on the width/height of the puzzle) into each empty square in such a way that no letter repeats in any row or column. Additionally, identical letters may not be in diagonally touching squares.

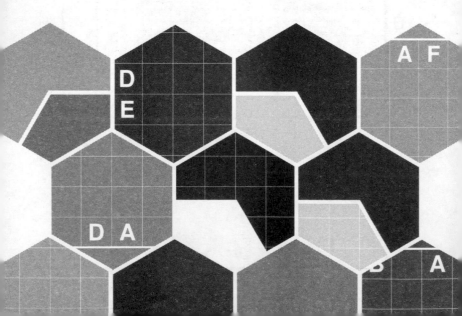

EXAMPLE

	C	A		F		
G						D
			F			
F		C		A		B
			E			
E						A
	D		B		E	

SOLUTION

B	C	G	A	D	F	E
G	F	E	C	B	A	D
A	B	D	F	E	C	G
F	E	C	G	A	D	B
D	A	B	E	F	G	C
E	G	F	D	C	B	A
C	D	A	B	G	E	F

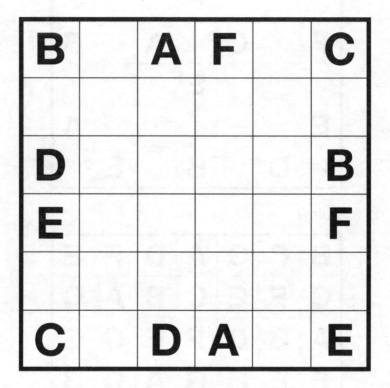

SOLUTION SEE PAGE 277

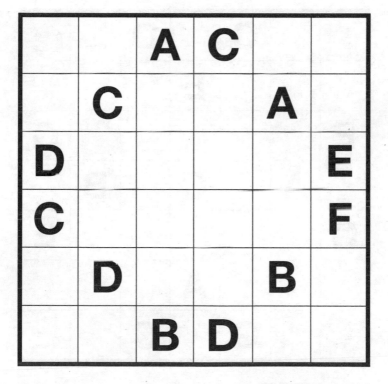

SOLUTION SEE PAGE 277

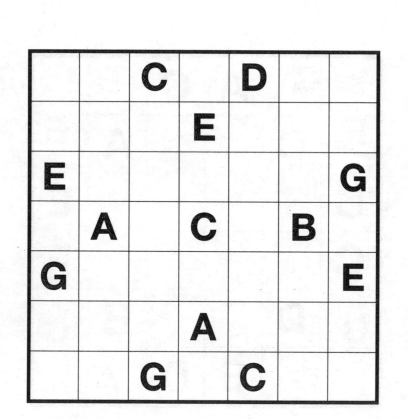

SOLUTION SEE PAGE 278

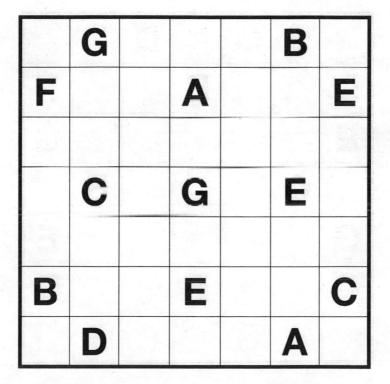

SOLUTION SEE PAGE 278

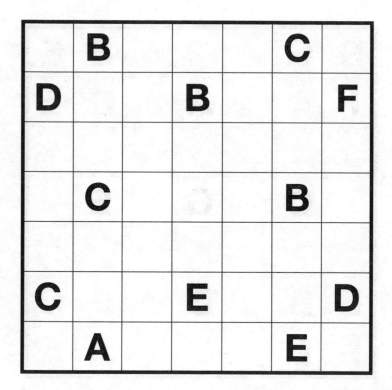

SOLUTION SEE PAGE 279

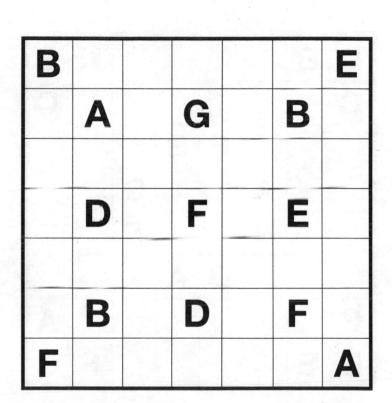

SOLUTION SEE PAGE 279

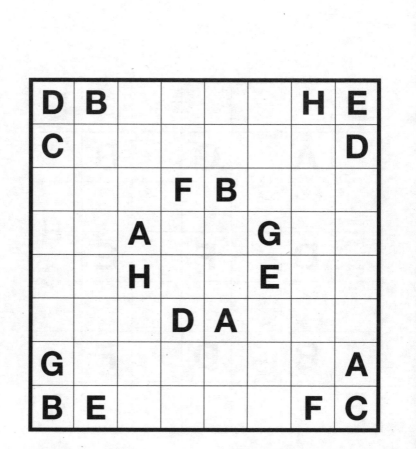

SOLUTION SEE PAGE 280

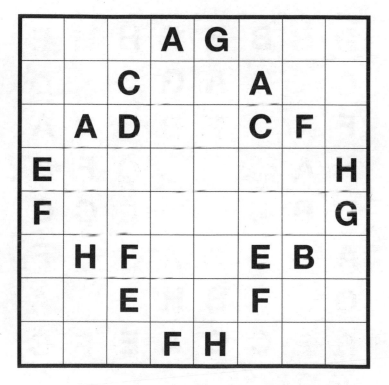

SOLUTION SEE PAGE 280

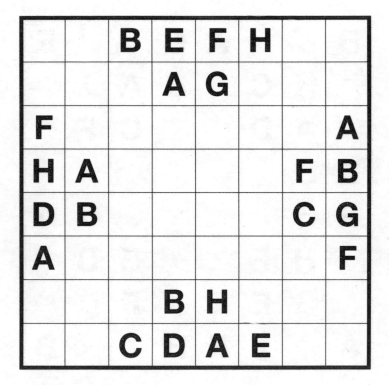

SOLUTION SEE PAGE 281

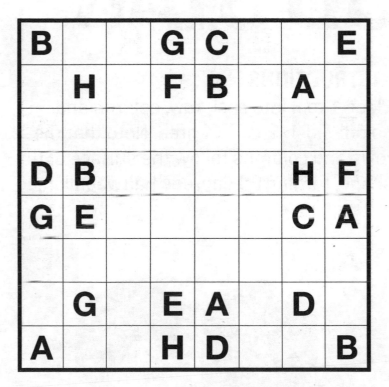

B			G	C			E
	H		F	B		A	
D	B					H	F
G	E					C	A
	G		E	A		D	
A			H	D			B

SOLUTION SEE PAGE 281

SUDOKU
3D STAR

INSTRUCTIONS

Place 1 to 8 into each row, column and bold-lined 4×2 or 2×4 area. Note that the rows and columns follow the surface of the shape, turning 90 degrees halfway along.

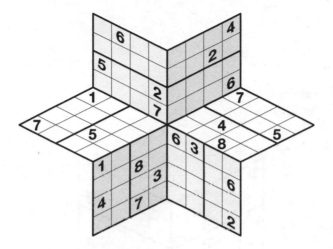

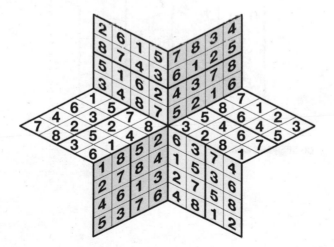

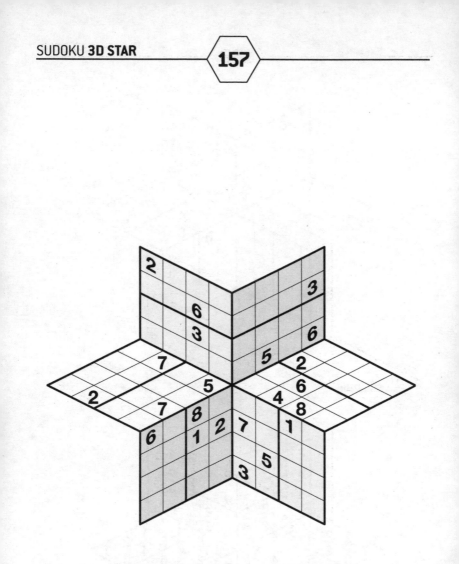

SOLUTION SEE PAGE 282

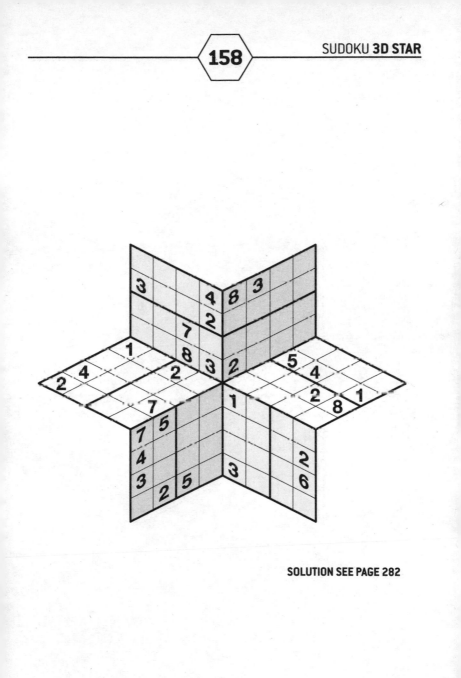

SOLUTION SEE PAGE 282

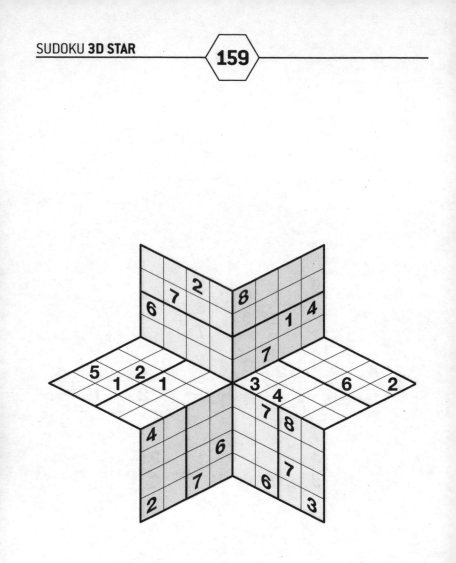

SOLUTION SEE PAGE 283

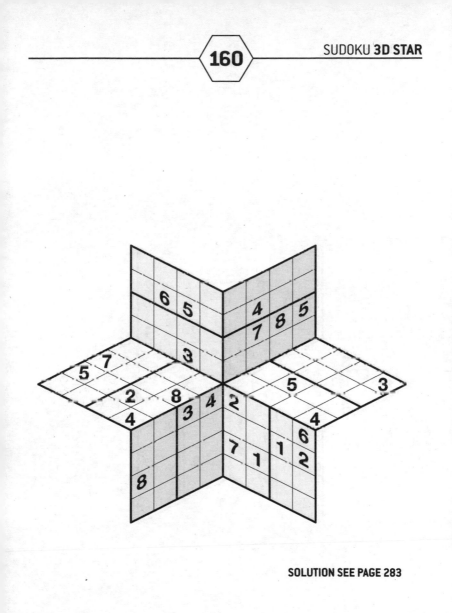

SOLUTION SEE PAGE 283

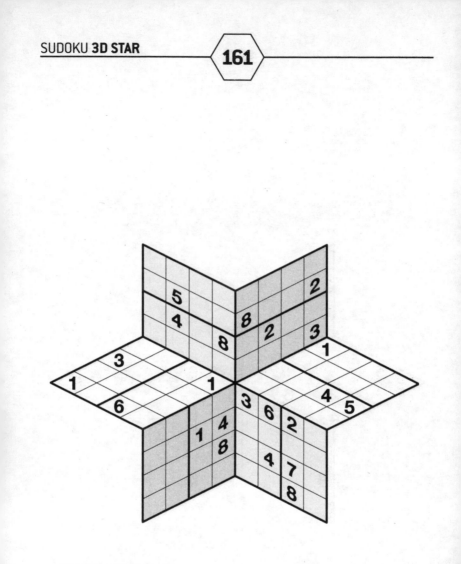

SOLUTION SEE PAGE 284

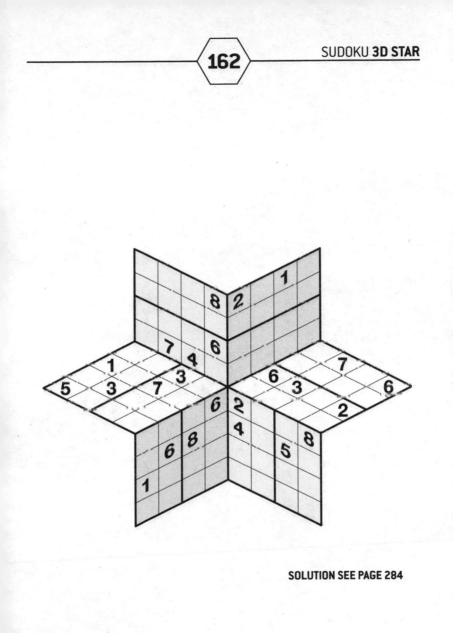

SOLUTION SEE PAGE 284

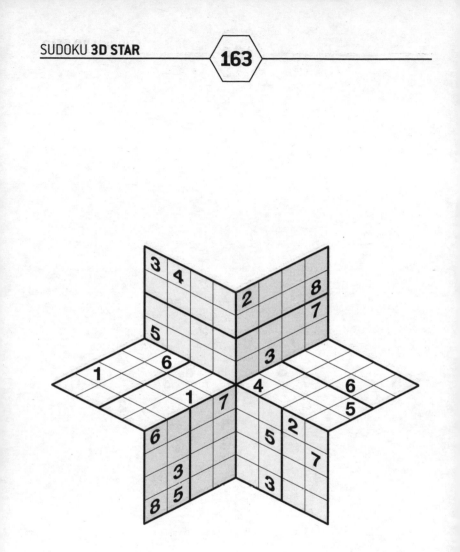

SOLUTION SEE PAGE 285

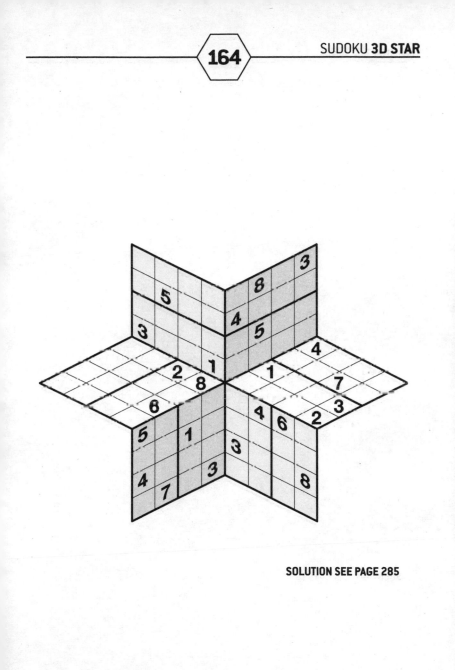

SOLUTION SEE PAGE 285

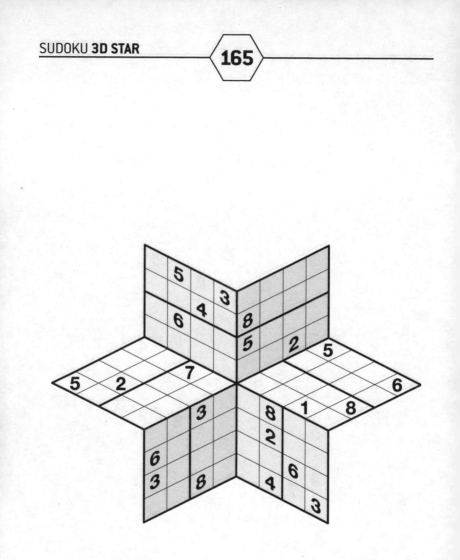

SOLUTION SEE PAGE 286

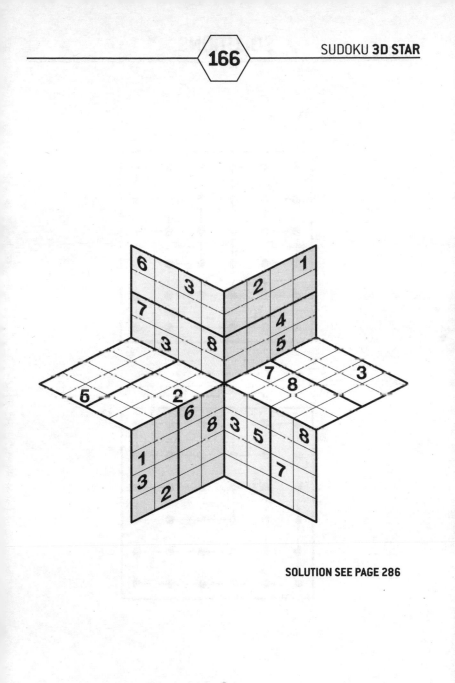

SOLUTION SEE PAGE 286

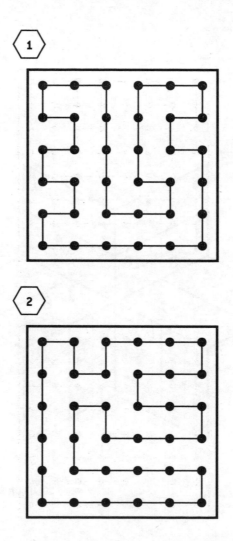

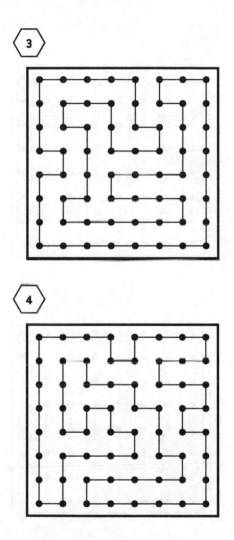

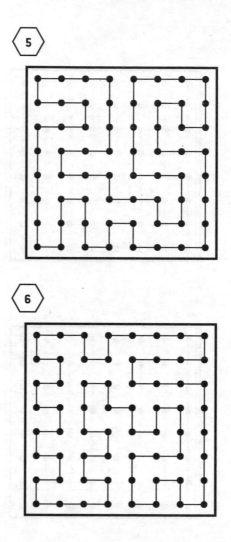

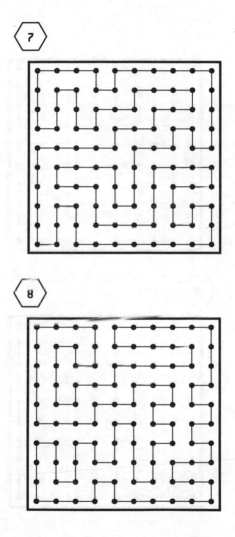

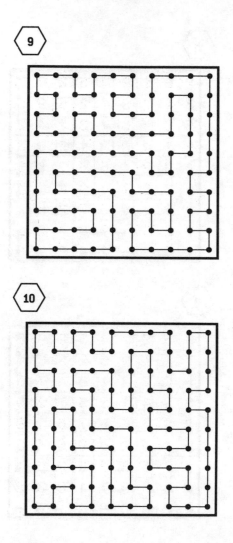

11

2	6	1	9	4	5	3	8	7
3	4	7	8	1	2	6	9	5
5	8	9	6	7	3	1	4	2
9	7	4	2	3	1	5	6	8
1	2	8	4	5	6	7	3	9
6	3	5	7	8	9	2	1	4
4	9	2	3	6	7	8	5	1
7	5	3	1	9	8	4	2	6
8	1	6	5	2	4	9	7	3

12

8	5	1	7	4	3	2	9	6
7	4	6	9	5	2	3	8	1
9	3	2	8	1	6	4	7	5
6	8	4	1	3	5	7	2	9
2	9	3	4	6	7	5	1	8
5	1	7	2	8	9	6	4	3
1	7	5	3	2	8	9	6	4
4	6	9	5	7	1	8	3	2
3	2	8	6	9	4	1	5	7

SOLUTIONS

13

7	6	8	1	2	4	9	5	3
9	2	3	5	8	6	7	1	4
1	4	5	7	3	9	6	2	8
8	7	2	6	5	1	3	4	9
5	3	4	8	9	7	1	6	2
6	1	9	3	4	2	8	7	5
3	9	1	4	6	5	2	8	7
2	5	6	9	7	8	4	3	1
4	8	7	2	1	3	5	9	6

14

5	3	9	6	2	4	1	8	7
4	8	6	1	5	7	2	9	3
2	1	7	3	9	8	6	4	5
9	4	3	5	7	2	8	6	1
7	2	5	8	1	6	9	3	4
8	6	1	4	3	9	7	5	2
3	9	2	7	6	5	4	1	8
6	5	4	2	8	1	3	7	9
1	7	8	9	4	3	5	2	6

15

5	1	6	9	3	2	8	7	4
4	7	3	5	8	1	2	6	9
2	8	9	4	6	7	3	1	5
8	6	7	3	2	4	5	9	1
3	5	1	7	9	6	4	8	2
9	2	4	8	1	5	6	3	7
7	3	2	6	5	9	1	4	8
1	9	8	2	4	3	7	5	6
6	4	5	1	7	8	9	2	3

16

5	3	8	9	2	6	7	4	1
6	7	2	8	4	1	3	5	9
4	1	9	7	5	3	2	8	6
7	8	1	6	3	9	4	2	5
9	4	5	1	7	2	8	6	3
3	2	6	5	8	4	9	1	7
1	6	4	3	9	8	5	7	2
2	9	7	4	6	5	1	3	8
8	5	3	2	1	7	6	9	4

SOLUTIONS

8	9	6	4	7	5	2	1	3
4	7	1	2	3	8	6	5	9
5	2	3	6	9	1	8	7	4
9	3	7	8	5	4	1	6	2
2	8	4	7	1	6	9	3	5
1	6	5	9	2	3	7	4	8
6	4	9	3	8	7	5	2	1
3	5	8	1	6	2	4	9	7
7	1	2	5	4	9	3	8	6

7	9	8	1	4	6	2	5	3
5	2	1	3	8	7	6	4	9
4	6	3	2	5	9	7	1	8
1	3	5	7	6	8	9	2	4
8	4	9	5	1	2	3	6	7
6	7	2	4	9	3	5	8	1
3	1	7	8	2	5	4	9	6
2	8	6	9	7	4	1	3	5
9	5	4	6	3	1	8	7	2

8	1	6	4	7	2	5	3	9
2	9	7	1	3	5	8	4	6
5	4	3	8	6	9	2	1	7
1	8	9	2	4	6	3	7	5
7	6	5	9	1	3	4	8	2
4	3	2	7	5	8	6	9	1
6	7	1	5	8	4	9	2	3
3	2	4	6	9	7	1	5	8
9	5	8	3	2	1	7	6	4

7	5	8	6	1	9	2	4	3
9	4	3	2	7	8	6	5	1
2	6	1	4	5	3	7	9	8
8	3	6	9	2	7	5	1	4
5	2	9	1	4	6	3	8	7
4	1	7	8	3	5	9	2	6
3	9	5	7	8	1	4	6	2
1	7	2	5	6	4	8	3	9
6	8	4	3	9	2	1	7	5

21

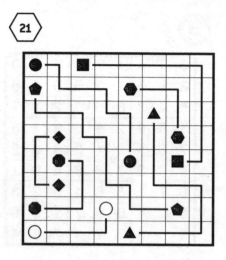

22

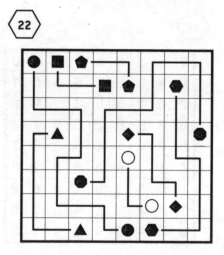

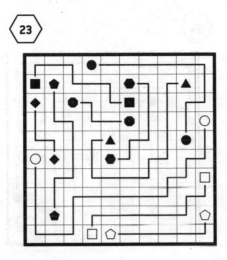

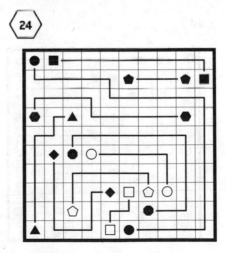

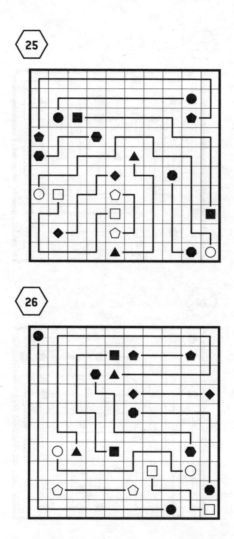

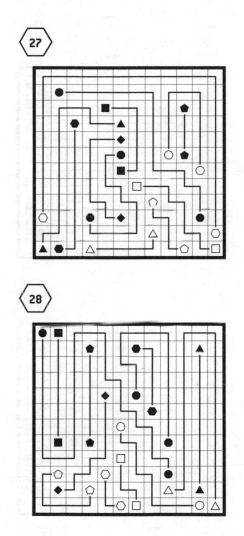

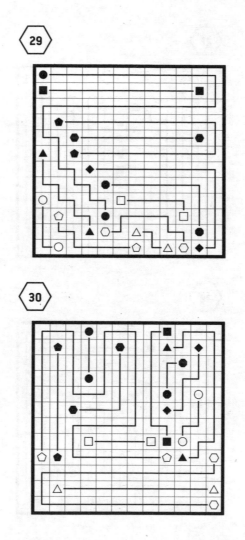

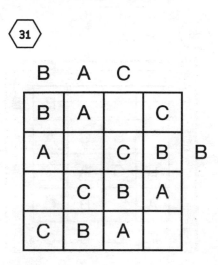

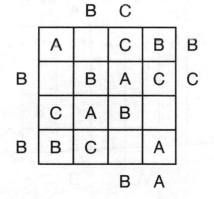

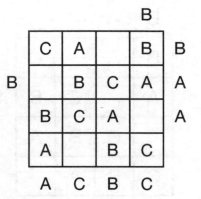

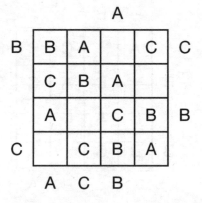

35

	B			B	
A	B	C			C
C			A	B	B
		A	B	C	C
A	A	B	C		
B	C			A	
	B		B	C	

36

	A					
C		C		B	A	A
A	A	B	C			C
A			A	C	B	B
	C		B	A		A
B	B	A			C	
	B	A	B		C	

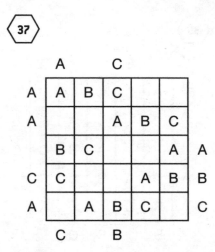

Puzzle 37:

	A		C			
A	A	B	C			
A			A	B	C	
	B	C			A	A
C	C			A	B	B
A		A	B	C		C
		C		B		

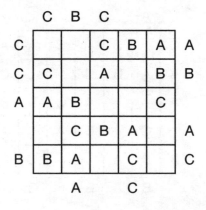

Puzzle 38:

	C	B	C			
C			C	B	A	A
C	C		A		B	B
A	A	B			C	
		C	B	A		A
B	B	A		C		C
		A		C		

39

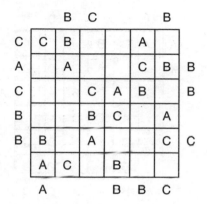

	B	C			B	
C	C	B			A	
A		A			C	B	B
C			C	A	B		B
B			B	C		A	
B	B		A			C	C
	A	C		B			
	A			B	B	C

40

	C	A	C	B		
A			A	C	B	
			B	A	C		C
B	B	C				A	A
C	C	A				B	B
A	A	B				C	C
C			C	B	A		A
	A				C	

41

	D	C			D		
	D	C	B			A	A
A			A	C	D	B	
	C		D	B	A		A
	B	A	C	D			D
	A	D			B	C	
B		B		A	C	D	D
		B	C	A	C	D	

42

	A	C	D	C	C		
	A		D	C		B	
A			A	B	C	D	D
	B	C		D	A		A
	C	D		A	B		B
D	D	A	B			C	C
		B	C		D	A	A
		C	A	D			

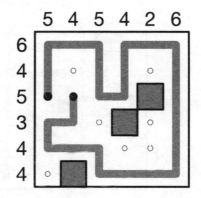

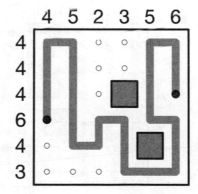

SOLUTIONS

45

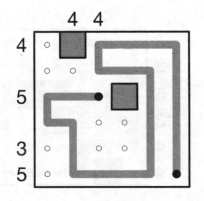

46

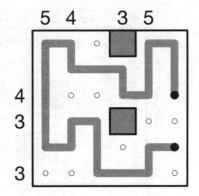

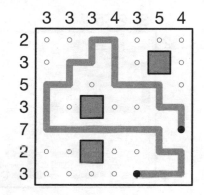

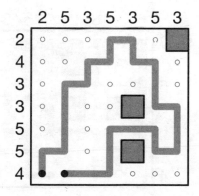

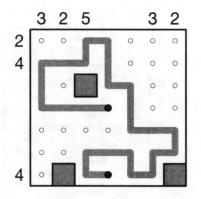

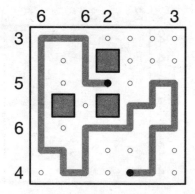

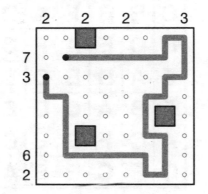

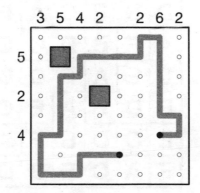

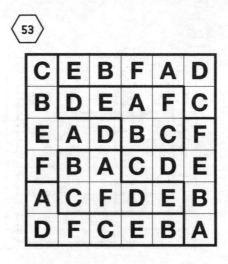

53

C	E	B	F	A	D
B	D	E	A	F	C
E	A	D	B	C	F
F	B	A	C	D	E
A	C	F	D	E	B
D	F	C	E	B	A

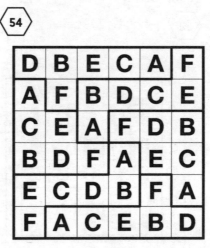

54

D	B	E	C	A	F
A	F	B	D	C	E
C	E	A	F	D	B
B	D	F	A	E	C
E	C	D	B	F	A
F	A	C	E	B	D

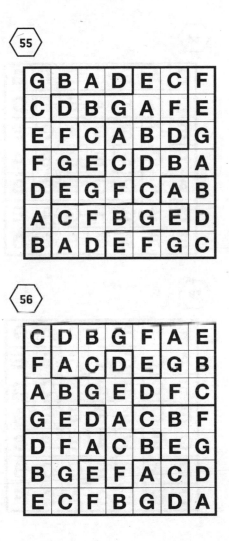

55

G	B	A	D	E	C	F
C	D	B	G	A	F	E
E	F	C	A	B	D	G
F	G	E	C	D	B	A
D	E	G	F	C	A	B
A	C	F	B	G	E	D
B	A	D	E	F	G	C

56

C	D	B	G	F	A	E
F	A	C	D	E	G	B
A	B	G	E	D	F	C
G	E	D	A	C	B	F
D	F	A	C	B	E	G
B	G	E	F	A	C	D
E	C	F	B	G	D	A

57

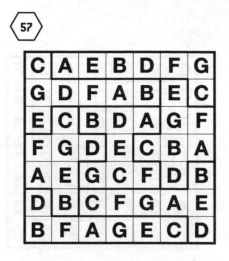

C	A	E	B	D	F	G
G	D	F	A	B	E	C
E	C	B	D	A	G	F
F	G	D	E	C	B	A
A	E	G	C	F	D	B
D	B	C	F	G	A	E
B	F	A	G	E	C	D

58

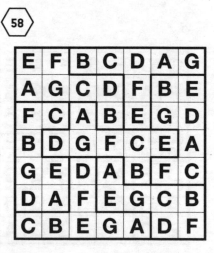

E	F	B	C	D	A	G
A	G	C	D	F	B	E
F	C	A	B	E	G	D
B	D	G	F	C	E	A
G	E	D	A	B	F	C
D	A	F	E	G	C	B
C	B	E	G	A	D	F

59

B	D	C	H	F	G	A	E
D	E	G	A	B	F	H	C
F	A	H	C	E	D	B	G
H	F	E	D	G	B	C	A
C	G	A	B	D	E	F	H
A	B	F	E	H	C	G	D
G	H	D	F	C	A	E	B
E	C	B	G	A	H	D	F

60

G	H	A	C	F	B	D	E
E	D	F	B	C	H	G	A
A	C	B	D	H	G	E	F
H	G	E	F	A	D	C	B
B	A	C	E	D	F	H	G
D	F	H	A	G	E	B	C
C	E	G	H	B	A	F	D
F	B	D	G	E	C	A	H

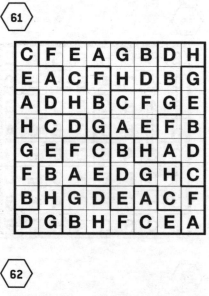

61

C	F	E	A	G	B	D	H
E	A	C	F	H	D	B	G
A	D	H	B	C	F	G	E
H	C	D	G	A	E	F	B
G	E	F	C	B	H	A	D
F	B	A	E	D	G	H	C
B	H	G	D	E	A	C	F
D	G	B	H	F	C	E	A

62

H	B	D	A	F	C	E	G
C	G	F	D	E	H	A	B
F	A	G	E	B	D	C	H
E	H	C	B	A	G	D	F
B	E	H	G	C	A	F	D
A	D	B	F	H	E	G	C
D	F	A	C	G	B	H	E
G	C	E	H	D	F	B	A

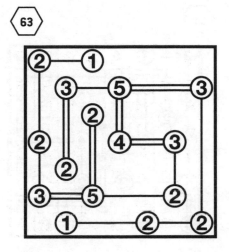

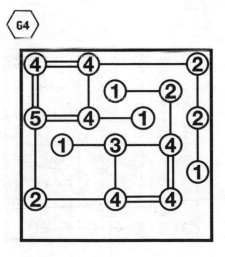

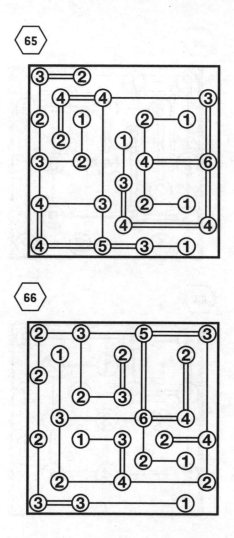

67

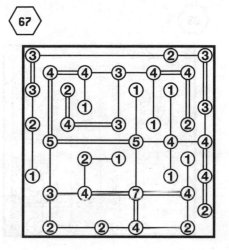

68

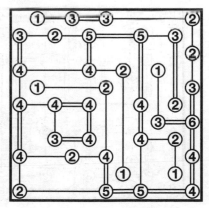

SOLUTIONS

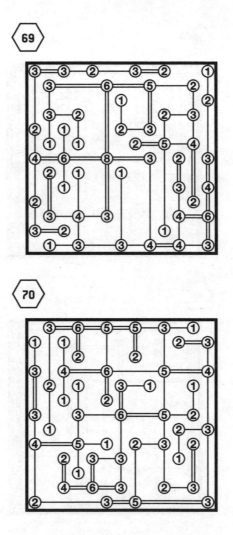

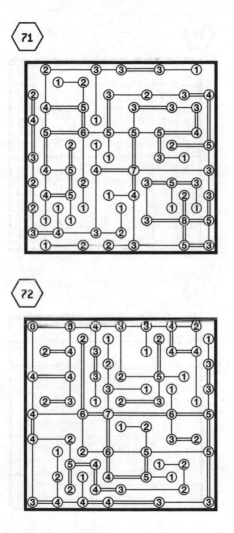

0	0	1	0	1	0	1	1
0	0	1	0	1	0	1	1
1	1	0	1	0	1	0	0
0	0	1	0	1	1	0	1
1	1	0	1	0	0	1	0
0	0	1	0	1	1	0	1
1	1	0	1	0	1	0	0
1	1	0	1	0	0	1	0

1	0	0	1	0	0	1	1
1	0	0	1	0	0	1	1
0	1	1	0	1	1	0	0
1	0	0	1	0	0	1	1
0	1	1	0	1	1	0	0
0	0	1	0	1	0	1	1
1	1	0	1	0	1	0	0
0	1	1	0	1	1	0	0

SOLUTIONS

⟨75⟩

0	0	1	0	1	0	1	1
1	0	0	1	0	0	1	1
0	1	1	0	1	1	0	0
0	0	1	0	1	0	1	1
1	1	0	1	0	1	0	0
0	0	1	0	1	0	1	1
1	1	0	1	0	1	0	0
1	1	0	1	0	1	0	0

⟨76⟩

0	0	1	0	1	1	0	1
0	0	1	1	0	1	1	0
1	1	0	0	1	0	1	0
0	0	1	1	0	1	0	1
1	1	0	0	1	0	0	1
0	1	1	0	0	1	1	0
1	0	0	1	1	0	0	1
1	1	0	1	0	0	1	0

0	0	1	0	0	1	1	0	1	1
1	0	0	1	0	1	1	0	0	1
0	1	1	0	1	0	0	1	1	0
0	0	1	0	0	1	1	0	1	1
1	0	0	1	1	0	0	1	0	1
1	1	0	1	0	0	1	0	1	0
0	1	1	0	1	1	0	1	0	0
0	0	1	0	0	1	1	0	1	1
1	1	0	1	1	0	0	1	0	0
1	1	0	1	1	0	0	1	0	0

0	0	1	0	0	1	1	0	1	1
0	0	1	0	0	1	1	0	1	1
1	1	0	1	1	0	0	1	0	0
0	0	1	0	1	0	1	0	1	1
0	0	1	1	0	1	0	1	0	1
1	1	0	1	0	0	1	1	0	0
1	1	0	0	1	1	0	0	1	0
0	0	1	0	1	0	1	1	0	1
1	1	0	1	0	1	0	0	1	0
1	1	0	1	1	0	0	1	0	0

SOLUTIONS

1	0	0	1	0	0	1	0	1	1
1	0	0	1	0	1	0	1	1	0
0	1	1	0	1	0	1	0	0	1
0	0	1	1	0	0	1	1	0	1
1	0	0	1	0	1	0	1	1	0
0	1	1	0	1	0	1	0	0	1
0	1	0	0	1	1	0	1	1	0
1	0	1	1	0	0	1	0	0	1
0	1	1	0	1	1	0	0	1	0
1	1	0	0	1	1	0	1	0	0

80

1	0	0	1	0	0	1	1	0	1
0	0	1	0	0	1	1	0	1	1
0	1	1	0	1	0	0	1	1	0
1	0	0	1	1	0	1	0	0	1
0	1	1	0	0	1	1	0	1	0
0	0	1	0	1	1	0	1	0	1
1	1	0	1	1	0	0	1	0	0
0	0	1	1	0	1	1	0	1	0
1	1	0	0	1	0	0	1	0	1
1	1	0	1	0	1	0	0	1	0

1	0	0	1	0	1	0	0	1	1	0	1
0	1	0	0	1	0	0	1	1	0	1	1
0	0	1	0	1	0	1	1	0	1	1	0
1	0	1	1	0	1	0	0	1	0	0	1
0	1	0	1	0	0	1	0	1	0	1	1
0	0	1	0	1	0	1	1	0	1	1	0
1	1	0	0	1	1	0	1	0	1	0	0
0	1	0	1	0	0	1	0	1	0	1	1
1	0	1	0	1	1	0	1	0	1	0	0
0	1	1	0	1	0	1	1	0	0	1	0
1	1	0	1	0	1	0	0	1	0	0	1
1	0	1	1	0	1	1	0	0	1	0	0

0	0	1	1	0	0	1	0	1	1	0	1
0	0	1	1	0	1	0	1	0	1	1	0
1	1	0	0	1	0	0	1	0	0	1	1
0	0	1	0	1	0	1	0	1	1	0	1
0	0	1	1	0	1	0	1	1	0	1	0
1	1	0	0	1	0	0	1	0	0	1	1
1	0	0	1	0	1	1	0	1	1	0	0
0	1	1	0	0	1	0	0	1	0	1	1
1	1	0	0	1	0	1	1	0	1	0	0
0	0	1	1	0	1	1	0	1	0	0	1
1	1	0	0	1	1	0	1	0	0	1	0
1	1	0	1	1	0	1	0	0	1	0	0

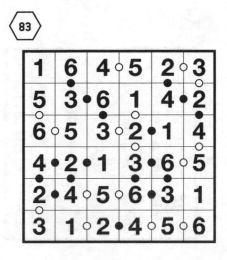

83

1	6	4	5	2	3
5	3	6	1	4	2
6	5	3	2	1	4
4	2	1	3	6	5
2	4	5	6	3	1
3	1	2	4	5	6

84

4	6	5	2	1	3
3	1	4	6	2	5
6	3	2	5	4	1
1	4	6	3	5	2
2	5	3	1	6	4
5	2	1	4	3	6

85

3	6	1	4	2	5	7
4	3	7	6	5	1	2
5	7	2	1	6	4	3
2	4	3	5	1	7	6
7	5	6	2	4	3	1
1	2	4	3	7	6	5
6	1	5	7	3	2	4

86

3	4	2	1	7	5	6
5	2	1	3	6	7	4
7	3	6	2	5	4	1
2	5	7	4	1	6	3
1	7	5	6	4	3	2
4	6	3	7	2	1	5
6	1	4	5	3	2	7

87

7	4	3	6	1	2	5
4	5	1	7	3	6	2
2	3	7	5	6	4	1
5	6	4	2	7	1	3
3	7	6	1	2	5	4
1	2	5	3	4	7	6
6	1	2	4	5	3	7

88

5	7	3	4	1	2	6
3	6	5	7	4	1	2
7	4	1	2	6	3	5
1	5	6	3	2	4	7
6	1	2	5	3	7	4
4	2	7	1	5	6	3
2	3	4	6	7	5	1

89

6	8	1	3	5	4	2	7
4	2	6	7	1	3	8	5
7	3	5	6	2	1	4	8
8	6	3	1	7	2	5	4
3	1	2	8	4	5	7	6
2	4	7	5	6	8	3	1
1	5	8	4	3	7	6	2
5	7	4	2	8	6	1	3

90

3	1	6	7	2	8	4	5
1	8	3	6	7	4	5	2
6	5	2	4	8	1	3	7
4	7	5	2	1	3	6	8
5	6	8	1	4	2	7	3
2	4	7	5	3	6	8	1
8	2	4	3	5	7	1	6
7	3	1	8	6	5	2	4

91

7	1	8	6	4	5	2	3
2	7	4	3	6	8	1	5
4	8	5	7	3	1	6	2
5	3	6	1	8	2	4	7
1	2	3	8	7	6	5	4
6	5	7	2	1	4	3	8
8	4	1	5	2	3	7	6
3	6	2	4	5	7	8	1

92

2	1	3	6	8	5	7	4
8	7	4	1	2	3	6	5
4	5	7	3	1	2	8	6
3	4	2	8	6	7	5	1
6	3	8	4	5	1	2	7
1	8	6	5	7	4	3	2
5	2	1	7	3	6	4	8
7	6	5	2	4	8	1	3

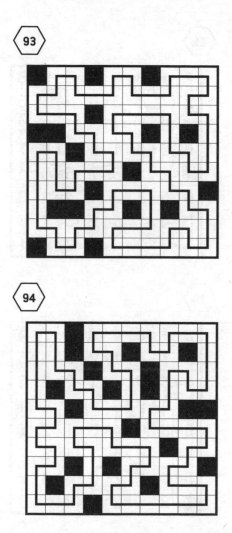

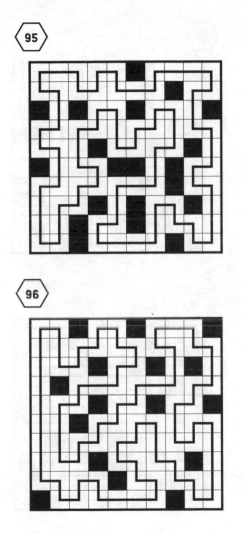

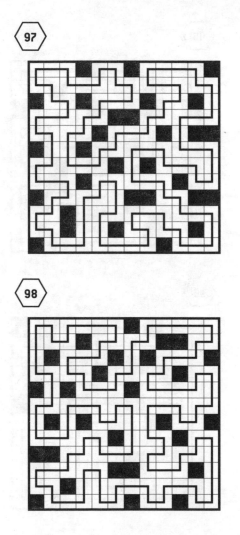

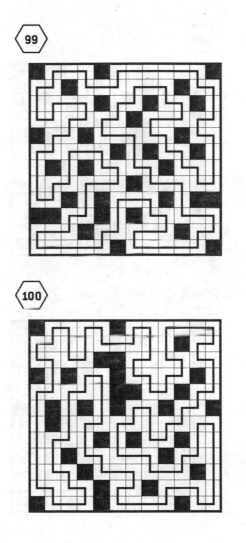

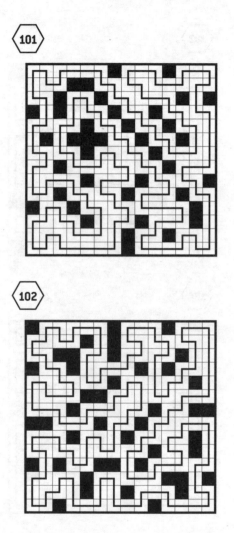

103

```
       3  4  2  2  1
    3 |3  1  2  4  5| 1
    3 |1  2  5  3  4| 2
    3 |2  4  1  5  3| 2
    2 |4  5  3  2  1| 4
    1 |5  3  4  1  2| 3
       1  2  2  3  4
```

104

```
       5  3
    3 |1  3  2  5  4|
      |2  1  5  4  3| 3
      |3  4  1  2  5|
      |4  5  3  1  2|
      |5  2  4  3  1| 4
```

105

	1	3	2	4	3	3	
1	6	3	5	1	4	2	4
2	4	2	6	3	1	5	2
5	2	1	3	4	5	6	1
3	3	5	4	6	2	1	3
2	5	6	1	2	3	4	2
4	1	4	2	5	6	3	2
	3	2	3	2	1	3	

106

	4		2	3			
	1	6	2	4	5	3	
3	3	5	1	2	4	6	
3	2	4	6	3	1	5	2
	5	2	3	1	6	4	2
	6	1	4	5	3	2	4
3	4	3	5	6	2	1	
		4			3	5	

107

	5						
	1	3	2	4	5	6	
3	2	1	4	3	6	5	
	3	4	6	5	1	2	3
	4	5	3	6	2	1	3
	6	2	5	1	4	3	4
	5	6	1	2	3	4	2
			3	2	3	3	

108

			4		3	2	
3	3	4	2	6	1	5	
	4	6	1	5	2	3	3
2	5	2	3	1	6	4	
	6	1	5	3	4	2	4
	1	5	4	2	3	6	1
	2	3	6	4	5	1	3
	2	3		3			

109

```
      5  5     4
   1  7  2  1  6  3  4  5  3
      5  3  2  7  4  6  1
   5  2  4  3  5  6  1  7
   2  6  1  5  3  7  2  4
      1  6  7  4  5  3  2  4
   2  3  7  4  1  2  5  6  2
   4  4  5  6  2  1  7  3
      3        4     1
```

110

```
         2  2  5  3
      4  7  6  5  1  3  2  5
   1  7  6  1  3  2  4  5  3
   2  5  3  2  1  4  7  6
   5  3  4  5  2  6  1  7
   4  1  2  3  7  5  6  4
      2  1  4  6  7  5  3
      6  5  7  4  3  2  1  5
      2           4  4
```

111

```
     1     3  2     3  3
   ┌──┬──┬──┬──┬──┬──┬──┐
   │ 7│ 6│ 4│ 2│ 1│ 3│ 5│ 3
   ├──┼──┼──┼──┼──┼──┼──┤
   │ 6│ 7│ 2│ 1│ 4│ 5│ 3│
   ├──┼──┼──┼──┼──┼──┼──┤
 3 │ 5│ 4│ 6│ 7│ 3│ 2│ 1│ 4
   ├──┼──┼──┼──┼──┼──┼──┤
 5 │ 2│ 1│ 3│ 4│ 5│ 7│ 6│
   ├──┼──┼──┼──┼──┼──┼──┤
 3 │ 4│ 5│ 1│ 3│ 7│ 6│ 2│
   ├──┼──┼──┼──┼──┼──┼──┤
 5 │ 1│ 3│ 5│ 6│ 2│ 4│ 7│
   ├──┼──┼──┼──┼──┼──┼──┤
   │ 3│ 2│ 7│ 5│ 6│ 1│ 4│
   └──┴──┴──┴──┴──┴──┴──┘
     5  4  1        4
```

112

```
     3     2  5
   ┌──┬──┬──┬──┬──┬──┬──┐
   │ 4│ 5│ 3│ 1│ 2│ 7│ 6│
   ├──┼──┼──┼──┼──┼──┼──┤
   │ 5│ 1│ 7│ 2│ 3│ 6│ 4│
   ├──┼──┼──┼──┼──┼──┼──┤
 1 │ 7│ 6│ 5│ 3│ 4│ 2│ 1│ 6
   ├──┼──┼──┼──┼──┼──┼──┤
   │ 6│ 2│ 1│ 4│ 7│ 5│ 3│
   ├──┼──┼──┼──┼──┼──┼──┤
 4 │ 1│ 4│ 6│ 7│ 5│ 3│ 2│ 4
   ├──┼──┼──┼──┼──┼──┼──┤
 2 │ 3│ 7│ 2│ 6│ 1│ 4│ 5│
   ├──┼──┼──┼──┼──┼──┼──┤
 6 │ 2│ 3│ 4│ 5│ 6│ 1│ 7│
   └──┴──┴──┴──┴──┴──┴──┘
     4              5
```

113

```
    3     6 1     2
  ┌───┬───┬───┬───┬───┬───┬───┐
  │ 5 │ 3 │ 1 │ 7 │ 2 │ 4 │ 6 │ 2
  ├───┼───┼───┼───┼───┼───┼───┤
  │ 6 │ 7 │ 2 │ 5 │ 3 │ 1 │ 4 │ 3
  ├───┼───┼───┼───┼───┼───┼───┤
  │ 7 │ 4 │ 3 │ 6 │ 5 │ 2 │ 1 │ 5
  ├───┼───┼───┼───┼───┼───┼───┤
3 │ 3 │ 6 │ 4 │ 2 │ 1 │ 7 │ 5 │
  ├───┼───┼───┼───┼───┼───┼───┤
5 │ 1 │ 2 │ 5 │ 3 │ 4 │ 6 │ 7 │
  ├───┼───┼───┼───┼───┼───┼───┤
  │ 2 │ 1 │ 7 │ 4 │ 6 │ 5 │ 3 │
  ├───┼───┼───┼───┼───┼───┼───┤
4 │ 4 │ 5 │ 6 │ 1 │ 7 │ 3 │ 2 │ 3
  └───┴───┴───┴───┴───┴───┴───┘
    2
```

114

```
    6 2
  ┌───┬───┬───┬───┬───┬───┬───┐
4 │ 1 │ 2 │ 6 │ 5 │ 4 │ 3 │ 7 │
  ├───┼───┼───┼───┼───┼───┼───┤
  │ 4 │ 1 │ 2 │ 3 │ 7 │ 6 │ 5 │ 3
  ├───┼───┼───┼───┼───┼───┼───┤
  │ 5 │ 3 │ 4 │ 7 │ 6 │ 2 │ 1 │ 4
  ├───┼───┼───┼───┼───┼───┼───┤
4 │ 3 │ 4 │ 5 │ 2 │ 1 │ 7 │ 6 │
  ├───┼───┼───┼───┼───┼───┼───┤
1 │ 7 │ 5 │ 3 │ 6 │ 2 │ 1 │ 4 │
  ├───┼───┼───┼───┼───┼───┼───┤
  │ 2 │ 6 │ 7 │ 1 │ 5 │ 4 │ 3 │ 4
  ├───┼───┼───┼───┼───┼───┼───┤
  │ 6 │ 7 │ 1 │ 4 │ 3 │ 5 │ 2 │ 3
  └───┴───┴───┴───┴───┴───┴───┘
              3   4       5
```

115

116

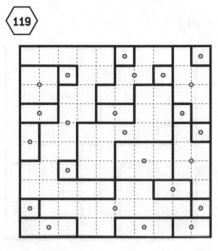

119

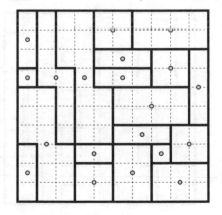

120

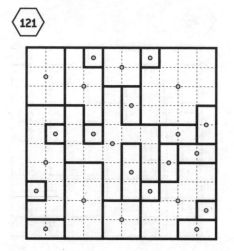

121

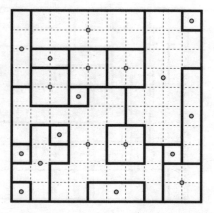

122

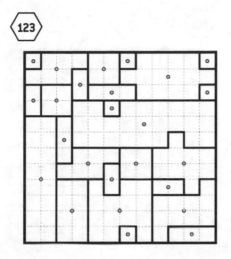

123

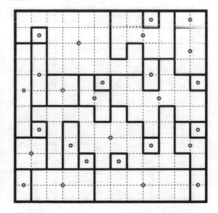

124

7	4	1	5	2	6	9	8	3
9	5	3	8	4	1	2	7	6
2	6	8	9	7	3	1	5	4
6	8	4	3	1	7	5	9	2
5	1	2	6	9	4	7	3	8
3	9	7	2	8	5	4	6	1
4	7	9	1	3	8	6	2	5
8	2	6	4	5	9	3	1	7
1	3	5	7	6	2	8	4	9

3	6	8	5	1	9	7	4	2
1	9	5	7	4	2	3	8	6
4	2	7	3	6	8	5	9	1
2	1	3	4	8	6	9	5	7
7	8	6	1	9	5	2	3	4
5	4	9	2	7	3	1	6	8
9	3	4	8	2	7	6	1	5
8	5	2	6	3	1	4	7	9
6	7	1	9	5	4	8	2	3

9	4	2	7	6	3	8	5	1
5	6	3	1	8	9	7	4	2
1	8	7	4	5	2	6	3	9
2	5	8	3	4	6	1	9	7
7	1	9	8	2	5	3	6	4
4	3	6	9	7	1	5	2	8
3	7	4	6	9	8	2	1	5
6	9	5	2	1	7	4	8	3
8	2	1	5	3	4	9	7	6

8	9	4	5	6	7	3	2	1
1	2	6	3	8	9	4	5	7
5	3	7	4	2	1	8	9	6
7	4	9	2	3	8	1	6	5
6	8	2	1	7	5	9	4	3
3	5	1	9	4	6	7	8	2
4	1	3	8	5	2	6	7	9
9	6	5	7	1	4	2	3	8
2	7	8	6	9	3	5	1	4

129

1	3	5	2	9	4	8	6	7
7	6	2	8	1	3	9	4	5
4	8	9	6	5	7	1	2	3
8	1	4	7	2	5	3	9	6
6	9	3	4	8	1	5	7	2
5	2	7	3	6	9	4	8	1
2	5	6	9	3	8	7	1	4
9	4	1	5	7	6	2	3	8
3	7	8	1	4	2	6	5	9

130

1	9	6	7	8	2	5	3	4
2	3	8	1	5	4	6	7	9
7	4	5	9	3	6	8	1	2
6	7	4	8	1	5	2	9	3
5	8	1	3	2	9	4	6	7
9	2	3	4	6	7	1	8	5
3	6	2	5	7	1	9	4	8
8	1	9	2	4	3	7	5	6
4	5	7	6	9	8	3	2	1

131

9	5	1	6	3	4	7	2	8
4	6	7	1	2	8	9	5	3
2	8	3	7	9	5	4	6	1
5	1	9	2	4	7	3	8	6
6	7	8	5	1	3	2	9	4
3	2	4	8	6	9	5	1	7
7	9	5	4	8	1	6	3	2
8	4	2	3	5	6	1	7	9
1	3	6	9	7	2	8	4	5

132

6	4	7	8	5	1	9	3	2
2	1	3	9	4	6	7	5	8
5	8	9	7	3	2	4	1	6
3	6	1	5	9	4	8	2	7
8	5	4	2	7	3	1	6	9
7	9	2	6	1	8	5	4	3
9	3	8	4	6	5	2	7	1
4	7	6	1	2	9	3	8	5
1	2	5	3	8	7	6	9	4

9	4	6	3	7	1	8	2	5
5	3	8	4	9	2	7	1	6
7	1	2	8	6	5	3	9	4
3	9	7	5	4	6	2	8	1
6	2	4	7	1	8	5	3	9
1	8	5	9	2	3	4	6	7
4	5	1	2	8	9	6	7	3
2	7	9	6	3	4	1	5	8
8	6	3	1	5	7	9	4	2

7	1	8	4	6	3	9	2	5
5	3	4	9	7	2	1	8	6
6	2	9	5	1	8	7	3	4
3	7	1	6	8	4	5	9	2
4	8	5	1	2	9	3	6	7
9	6	2	7	3	5	4	1	8
1	9	6	2	5	7	8	4	3
2	5	3	8	4	1	6	7	9
8	4	7	3	9	6	2	5	1

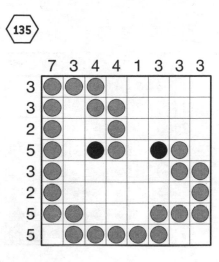

135

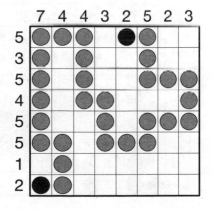

136

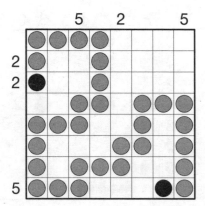

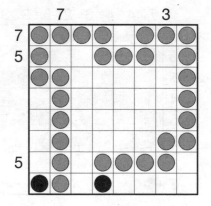

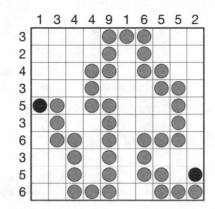

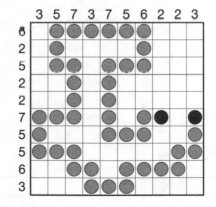

SOLUTIONS

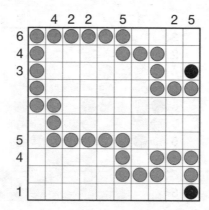

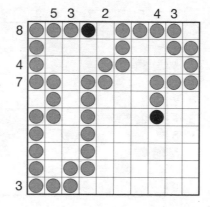

SOLUTIONS

143

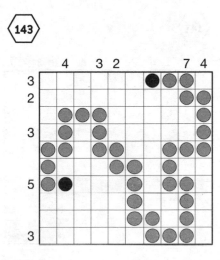

144

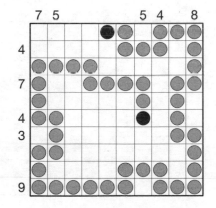

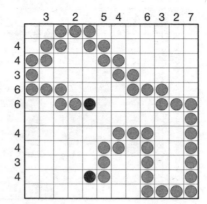

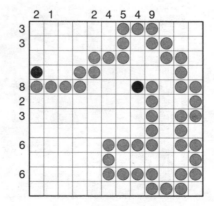

147

B	D	A	F	E	C
F	E	C	B	D	A
D	A	F	E	C	B
E	C	B	D	A	F
A	F	E	C	B	D
C	B	D	A	F	E

148

B	E	A	C	F	D
F	C	D	E	A	B
D	A	F	B	C	E
C	B	E	A	D	F
E	D	C	F	B	A
A	F	B	D	E	C

149

A	F	C	G	D	E	B
C	G	A	E	B	F	D
E	B	D	F	A	C	G
D	A	E	C	G	B	F
G	C	B	D	F	A	E
B	D	F	A	E	G	C
F	E	G	B	C	D	A

150

C	G	D	F	E	B	A
F	B	C	A	D	G	E
G	A	E	B	F	C	D
D	C	F	G	A	E	B
A	E	B	D	C	F	G
B	F	A	E	G	D	C
E	D	G	C	B	A	F

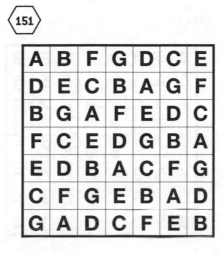

151

A	B	F	G	D	C	E
D	E	C	B	A	G	F
B	G	A	F	E	D	C
F	C	E	D	G	B	A
E	D	B	A	C	F	G
C	F	G	E	B	A	D
G	A	D	C	F	E	B

152

B	C	D	A	F	G	E
D	A	F	G	E	B	C
G	E	B	C	D	A	F
C	D	A	F	G	E	B
A	F	G	E	B	C	D
E	B	C	D	A	F	G
F	G	E	B	C	D	A

SOLUTIONS

153

D	B	F	A	G	C	H	E
C	A	G	H	E	F	B	D
E	D	C	F	B	H	A	G
H	F	A	E	D	G	C	B
A	G	H	B	C	E	D	F
F	C	E	D	A	B	G	H
G	H	B	C	F	D	E	A
B	E	D	G	H	A	F	C

154

C	E	H	A	G	B	D	F
H	F	C	B	D	A	G	E
G	A	D	H	E	C	F	B
E	B	G	C	F	D	A	H
F	D	A	E	B	H	C	G
A	H	F	G	C	E	B	D
B	G	E	D	A	F	H	C
D	C	B	F	H	G	E	A

155

G	C	B	E	F	H	A	D
E	H	F	A	G	D	B	C
F	D	G	H	B	C	E	A
H	A	E	C	D	G	F	B
D	B	H	F	E	A	C	G
A	E	D	G	C	B	H	F
C	G	A	B	H	F	D	E
B	F	C	D	A	E	G	H

156

B	D	A	G	C	H	F	E
C	H	E	F	B	G	A	D
E	F	D	A	H	C	B	G
D	B	G	C	E	A	H	F
G	E	H	B	F	D	C	A
F	A	C	D	G	B	E	H
H	G	B	E	A	F	D	C
A	C	F	H	D	E	G	B

⟨157⟩

⟨158⟩

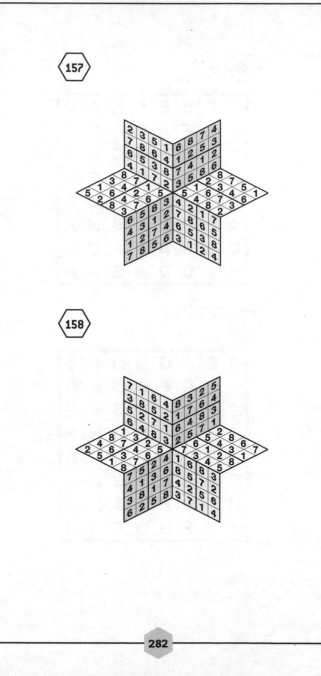

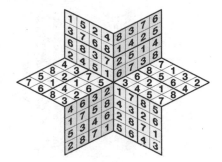

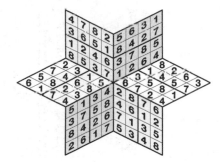

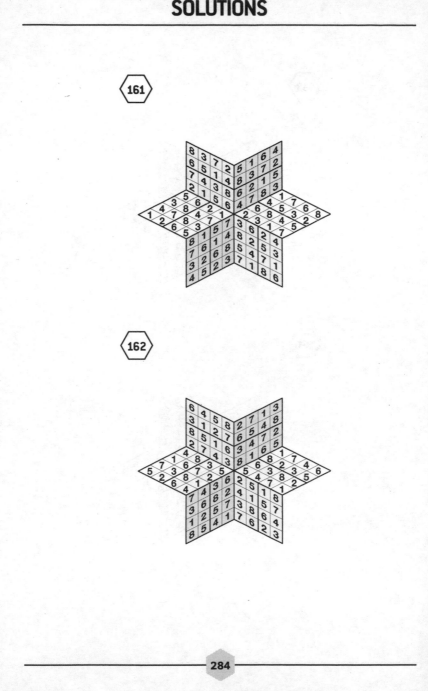

163

164

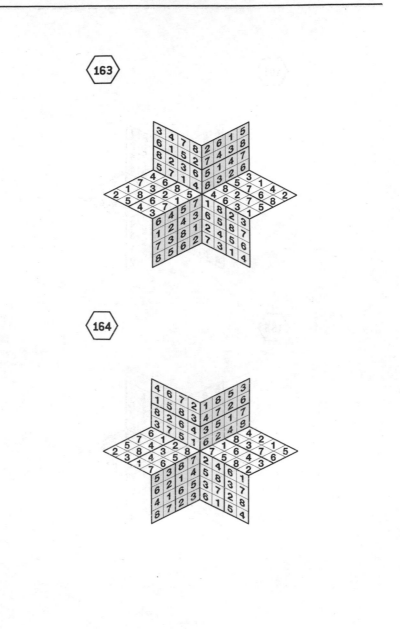

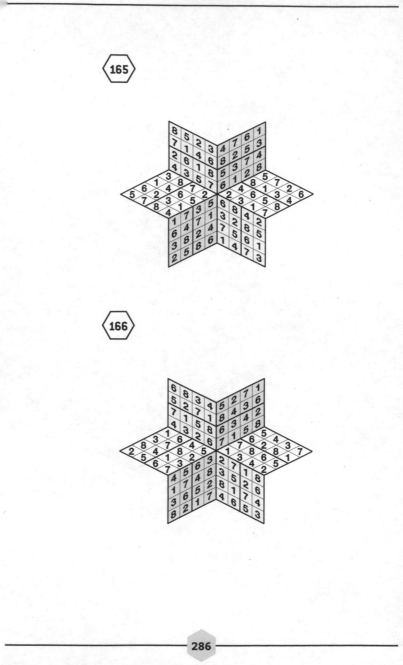

NOTES

NOTES